One-Eyed Kings

Lessons I Learned From an Incurable Disease

One-Eyed Kings

Lessons I Learned
From an Incurable Disease

James V. McTevia

with Tom W. Ferguson

Manufactured in the United States of America

Cover and interior design by Jacinta Calcut,
Image Graphics & Design, www.image-gd.com

Cover photograph by Chris Herbert

Published by Highlandview Farms
1028 N. Riverside Avenue
St. Clair, MI 48079
USA

ISBN 978-0-692-12342-3

Library of Congress Control Number: 2018944243

This book is dedicated to all those
who have discovered, or will discover,
that adversity is best met
one day at a time.

Contents

PROLOGUE

❧

ABOUT 20,000 AMERICANS are living with inclusion body myositis, a muscle disease that cannot, so far, be cured. Their peculiar disorder will worsen, a daunting fact of life for all who suffer what they and their doctors call IBM. Most IBM patients were blindsided by an adversary they had never heard of. As with many rare diseases, IBM lags in research resources because of its low profile.

Jim McTevia asked me to collaborate in telling his personal IBM story to help raise IBM's profile and offer encouragement to others facing what a friend of Jim's called "our damned disease." We hope the result, *One-Eyed Kings,* will inspire IBM victims, their loved ones, and readers facing any debilitating adversity.

Dr. Tom Lloyd leads a Johns Hopkins University medical and research team that has worked on the cutting edge of IBM science for a decade. Dr. Lloyd's afterword for *One-Eyed Kings* speaks to the other thousands of IBM patient stories here and abroad, to the promise of 21st Century medical research, and to the fascinating way human cells—our smallest common denominator—hold the key to so much knowledge and progress.

Life's voyage requires that each of us navigate our own storms. We hope Jim's travelogue from a journey in progress will be both a frank and inspiring companion.

Tom W. Ferguson
September 2018

1

Doing well and getting well

I remember gasping for breath that night as clearly as almost any moment of my life.

I WAS LIVING AT THE TOP OF THE WORLD. Figuratively speaking, of course. Not *the* top, up where the air is so rarefied that instead of buying tickets to fly on a jet plane, you buy a jet plane. Not even close. But I was rubbing elbows with some of those folks and I was inventing a profession that generated an excellent living. For a 40-year-old who skipped college and entered the workforce on a Great Lakes freighter, life in 1976 very often did feel as good as it could get. The truth on this particular night, however, was that I could not breathe. Gasping, I pushed myself out of bed, went to the window, cranked it open, sucked oxygen from the late-summer midnight breeze, and stared out over Lake Huron. Taking in fresh air was like adjusting the carburetor on an old Ford flathead V-8. In a few moments my body went back to running smoothly enough. Time to go back to bed, get some sleep, and head off to the office.

It was a scary moment. It should have been a teachable moment. But when you are young (40 *is* young, believe me) your learning is selective. Struggling for air in the middle of the night is not normal and not good. Common sense said I should visit a doctor. But my emerging profession tugged at my sleeve 24/7. It was teaching me life lessons every day. It made it possible for Joan, my wife of 20 years, and I to live on the shores of Lake Huron. My work was—most days and no small thing—*exciting*. Why would I steal even a few hours from this night-and-day vocation to go see a doctor? I mean, not only was I standing near the top of the world, I was immortal.

The readily observable facts suggested otherwise. At 40, I was more than 20 pounds overweight...a two-pack-a-day smoker...a guy who, as a professional with clients and prospective clients and associates to entertain, drank a bit too much, and ate too much food that cost a lot more than junk food but was not much more nutritious.

I got up early every morning. Some days Joan and I would drive south separately into Port Huron and meet for breakfast at a HoJo's where the I-94 freeway began—still 50 miles from the office and 60 miles from the downtown Detroit federal court where, in those days, I did a lot of work as a bankruptcy receiver. My deskwork got crammed between lunches and appointments, either downtown or back north at the McTevia & Associates office on Eight Mile Road. The firm by then employed some 40 associates at offices in three states, including Florida, where Joan and I kept a residence in Boca Raton. When working in Michigan, I would arrive back home at 8 or 9 p.m., study balance sheets and court documents for a while, get to bed around 11 or 11:30, and re-set the body clock for another day. A regular workweek meant almost no time for any semblance of a normal life.

I remember gasping for breath that night as clearly as almost any moment of my life. The teachable moment passed without teaching me anything. I remained a pudgy smoker whose cholesterol numbers no doubt should have alarmed me more than any client's shaky balance sheet. But no more oxygen emergencies occurred, and my work-obsessive routine changed not at all.

One day a business associate mentioned the Mayo Clinic and suggested I travel to the Minnesota cornfields for a Mayo Executive Health Program checkup. I paid no attention. Then, sometime in winter, Joan made a spring appointment for an exam. I would be going with her, so why not make an appointment for myself? My secretary made the phone call. It changed my life, and probably saved it.

The Mayo Clinic has ranked for generations among the world's top medical facilities. An endless procession of oil sheikhs, movie stars, celebrity athletes, CEOs, and world royalty—people with enough cash to seek treatment or surgery anywhere on earth—have chosen to do so on the eastern edge of America's great prairie in Rochester, Minnesota, population 114,000. One day Joan ran into evangelist Billy Graham. Several times on an elevator we encountered armed guards, part of some potentate's entourage. Paupers with health insurance vastly outnumber the visiting princes and the celebrities and the merely wealthy. Nonetheless, close encounters of the "I wonder who that is" kind become routine as you navigate

Mayo's assemblage of world-class physicians, scientists, nurses, and technicians.

Pilgrims arrive with every known disease, injury, and frailty. Many make their first trek, as I did in spring 1977, solely for a physical exam. In my case, two unexpected things happened. First, the Mayo doctors scared the hell out of me. Second, I've returned to Rochester every year since. That's 40 years of poking and prodding and imaging and surrendering fluids to the lab. It's no vacation, but I would not trade the two or three days a year at Mayo for two or three days a year on the beach.

It's hard to imagine any organization more efficient than the Mayo Clinic. Few entities— large or small, in any field—are even *as* efficient. Show up for a physical and you discover that referrals from an internist to a cardiologist to a neurologist to a rheumatologist are instantaneous, leading down the hall or up the elevator instead of across town a month later. Rather than waiting days for lab results, reports are completed while you are on the next leg of your medical tour. You are examined head-to-toe across all medical disciplines by doctors who are literally on the same page. At the end of the second or third day depending on any special circumstances, you sit down for a summing-up with the physician charged with bringing all those tests and specialty exams into focus.

The Mayo Clinic Executive Health Program became famous throughout the business world for its one-stop comprehensive approach to preventive medicine. I was by no means famous but I had become a highly specialized hero among companies whose fortunes turned hard south. Bankers and industrial credit managers and law firms and accountant firms began engaging me to deliver lectures while I was still in my 20s. As I founded and grew my consulting firm, more and more troubled companies, buried in debt and struggling, became my patients, so to speak. I slimmed down their operations so they could survive, or, if necessary, I took them through the end game of bankruptcy or liquidation. Ironically, it occurred to me while awaiting a doctor to sum up my Mayo visit, I had shepherded a hospital or two through the grim business of healing an unhealthy balance sheet. I report that history not to brag but for important context. That is to say, most of my "patients" came to me because a little success had made them begin to believe they were financially bulletproof. I was suffering the same delusion with my physical health.

After the doctor entered the room and began

analyzing my medical balance sheet, I no longer felt on the top of the world. I felt glad to be sitting down.

We had the usual brief small talk, and then he said: "You are a very impressive young man, but your health is not so very impressive."

That sort of thing catches your ear and travels straight to those parts of the brain where anxiety and dread gather steam.

He summed up the numbers and graphs that quantify heart and lung performance, cholesterol, muscle mass—all the body's usual sources of bad news for a middle-aged man. When these numbers are bad, the only good news is that once you get over the shock, you realize the bad news is what you paid to find out. The doctor gave me every penny's worth of bad news.

He promised me that in 10 years I would either be dead or impaired, incapacitated in not exactly predictable ways I definitely would not like. All this because I had allowed myself to become a slob. The doctor used medical and civil language. He did not say "slob." But with great clarity he made me realize, almost in an instant, that I was a poster boy for the impact of poor lifestyle choices—and that, yes, I was in a world-famous medical facility, but the most meaningful healing in this case was up to the patient. The Mayo Clinic is as good as it gets when it comes to fixing hearts and lungs and joints and other body parts that can be repaired. But doctors do not perform miracles, and doctors most definitely do not resurrect the dead, or even those who merely push fate in that direction. This very articulate physician told me I should pay as much attention to my health as I did to my business.

Fear is a great motivator. Besides, I have always believed that if something is doable, I can do it. I don't take challenges lightly, nor am I interested in challenges I can't win. That's one reason I never watch sports on TV, if you can follow the psychology. My grandkids' ballgames, sure. I've always been a sucker for that. But those jocks who get paid millions of dollars to hit a ball, or kick it, or throw it in a basket? I can't do any of those things myself, and if I wanted to do them I couldn't get significantly better by observing the best, so why watch? On the other hand, putting an end to being a slob was something I could do. Being dead in ten years was something I very much did not want to do. So I went all in on ceasing to be a slob.

The Marlboros went in the wastebasket, overnight and permanently. The cigars I enjoyed after a meal? I have to admit that after quitting for a bit I returned to that treasured habit for a dozen years, then quit again a decade or so ago.

Did I bid total farewell to demon rum, especially my favored Southern Comfort on the rocks, with just a kiss of vermouth and a lemon twist? No. But I cut alcohol consumption to the actual amount people confess when they fill out a medical questionnaire and call themselves "light drinkers." I am old enough to remember President Eisenhower's heart surgeon telling the world that a drink a day was good—and besides, I've never had a heart attack.

I began managing my nutrition and transforming myself from a 40-year-old who couldn't run down the driveway and up to the next corner. That was my starting point, my first benchmark. Before a year passed I became a regular and enthusiastic 10K competitor. More accurately, I became a 10K participant. I ran and finished, but I wasn't competing with anyone except myself. If you haven't tried this self-help path, I can vouch that going from a chain-smoking overweight desk jockey to a 10K runner, no matter how slow, is a great feeling. "Great" is an understatement. Eventually, after seeing fellow runners develop bad knees and other nagging or serious problems, I gave up running in favor of stationary bikes and treadmills. But I still have all those medals and ribbons that proclaim I showed up and went the distance. Nothing wrong with a little pride.

As you would expect, I began sleeping better. The workaholic in me became able to work even harder. I became a better person for my clients and, I hope, for everyone else. I have in fact viciously guarded my health ever since that day in 1977 when a Mayo Clinic doctor certified me as a sedentary businessman and a highly qualified prospect for the nearest enterprising undertaker.

Back in Minnesota for my annual physical in 1978, the staff reacted with various but considerable levels of disbelief. I had lost 20 pounds. I had some muscle. I passed, with flying colors, treadmill tests that 12 months earlier I had not been able to complete.

I was back on top of the world and feeling immortal again. No doubt about it.

2

THINGS TO DO, THINGS TO LEARN

*Tragedy lies in the hard-wired idea
that these things define someone, and there is
no way to face tomorrow without them.*

THE PARKING ATTENDANT NEEDED A SHAVE. He wore torn jeans and his shirt needed laundering. I was hurrying to leave the lot in downtown Miami and go meet a gaggle of news reporters awaiting me in Ft. Lauderdale. The attendant mustered no smile as I drove up to his booth, and he was indifferent about making eye contact. He was a 30-ish man enduring another day in a subsistence job while south Florida eased into the hot months of 1990. I was an important man doing important things, enjoying my customary place on top of the world. Such a comparison didn't cross my mind, of course. It didn't rise to the level of conscious thought. It must have been in my head somewhere, though, because in life's busy interactions we do act out our assigned roles, don't we?

The parking lot charged a reasonable hourly rate I have long forgotten and a flat rate I will never forget—20 dollars for anyone who claimed their car after 5 p.m., no matter what time it arrived. This should not have mattered. I could afford it. Besides, the parking fee was a reimbursable business expense. But I am a professional whose clients invariably need to do one of three things if they are going to have a chance of surviving. They can spend less money. Or they can generate more revenue. Or they can do both. "Both" is almost always their only path forward. Every day I read balance sheets where once great (or at least once viable) companies are revealed to have spent and borrowed themselves into the worst kind of trap. They hire me as their last resort. My job is to restructure operations, administer financial CPR, and get the company breathing again. One cannot do what I do all day and not take every expenditure seriously—even a parking fee, even when someone else is paying the bill.

I lowered the Town Car's window and handed the attendant my ticket. I had been in a nearby office holding a meeting related to my biggest case of the moment.

"No ticket," he said, and pointed to the lot's rate card. "After 5 o'clock."

It was indeed barely past the top of the hour. "Twenty dollars," the attendant said.

I was furious. Twenty bucks is, after all, twenty bucks. In 1990 it was more than twenty bucks. I pulled a $20 bill from my wallet and flung it toward the ticket booth's open window. This might have worked if I had wadded up the money. Instead, the bill sailed almost straight down into the narrow chasm separating car and booth, attendant and customer. We stared silently at each other in motionless stalemate.

So how did a guy from the Canadian border and a guy from the torrid tip of Florida wind up measuring each other across a physical divide measured by inches, but spanning such a wide strait of cultural and social differences? Pork bellies. Yes, pork bellies. Life is almost as interesting as it is precious.

I'll tell you the result of our standoff in a minute. First I need to brief you on the basics of my career, the thing that brought me to Miami in the first place. I know there is an elephant in the room—the book does say "incurable disease" on the cover. Trust me, that story will resonate much better if you first read one chapter about my six decades as a problem-solver. I don't think it's a spoiler to let you start pondering how "problem-solver" and "incurable" do not make a harmonious match.

Now, back to pork bellies and what I've been doing all these years. Then back to the parking lot impasse, which turned out to be far more important to me than 20 bucks.

Few investments are a bigger crapshoot than commodity futures, which amount to legal wagering on the future price of metals, energy, and agricultural products—including pork bellies. The possibility of big returns, though, can lure investors into almost any risk. If possible returns are portrayed as probable returns or even promised returns, a red line is crossed. Regulators sit up and take notice. The Commodity Futures Trading Commission took a look when customers of a south Florida futures trading company called MultiVest complained they had been promised, according to the Ft. Lauderdale *Sun-Sentinel*, double or triple their money in just a few days. The CFTC determined that about 13,000 MultiVest customers lost nearly $73 million from 1987 to 1989. While the feds decided what they could and should do next,

MultiVest's customers pursued a class action lawsuit. It was a massive financial mess that included the usual quota of personal tragedy.

In May 1990 a federal court appointed McTevia & Associates as permanent receiver, meaning I would be at the helm sailing Multi-Vest into the sunset. Company owners did not admit any guilt, but promised to do no wrong in the future. MultiVest customers went forward with their lawsuit. And I would be distributing what was left of a company that once employed several thousand people in five states. Remaining assets had to be liquidated for as much return as possible and shared equitably among all those with a claim against MultiVest. The story was huge in south Florida and a major business story across the country. I've had scores of more interesting cases and clients, but the sheer number of people damaged while thinking they were going to get rich quick made MultiVest unique. On some days that spring and summer, the MultiVest saga burned as hot as Miami pavement.

While MultiVest wound down I continued as I have through six calendar decades (now aiming for seven) to greet an endless stream of new clients. I don't need to advertise. Lawyers, accountants, and judges send cases my way. Word

of mouth has been strong among business owners and executives since before family cars had
seat belts. We have a vault of excellent press
clippings. Human nature guarantees a permanent supply of clients. People, businesses, and
governments all seem hell-bent on living in the
future—spending money they don't have, lock-
ing into future outlays they have no assurance
of being able to pay, borrowing unreasonable
and then outrageous sums of money so they can
dig ever deeper down a dark hole. My phone
rarely rings until a potential client, most often
the principal of a privately held company, can
neither burrow one inch deeper nor climb back
one inch toward fiscal sanity.

My professional immersion in the mechan-
ics, psychology, and consequences of unrealistic
debt began in 1957 at the most basic level. I
was sailing the Great Lakes as an ordinary seaman on the freighter SS Adam E. Cornelius. I
began my sailing career in a high-school summer job between 10th and 11th grade. But at age
19, in January 1957, I met Joan. In the spring
we became engaged, and in September we were
married. I had no formal education beyond high
school, and I wanted a job on dry land. When
you are young, need work, and are not predes-
tined or credentialed to pursue one career or

another, you look around and ask just two fundamental questions. First: "Will the paycheck bounce?" Second: "When can I start?"

And so, because I knew someone who worked there, three weeks before our wedding I found a job at the very bottom of lending's food chain, knocking on doors and collecting overdue payments on behalf of Doty Discount Finance Co. I soon moved up to reclaiming Crown Victorias and Super 88s from Detroit's streets and alleys. I was a repo man. Every workaholic day since then has been spent dealing one way or another with financial obligations gone bad or in danger of going bad. By starting on the streets of Detroit without a degree hanging on the wall, I earned a Ph.D. from the School of Important Things You Can't Learn Anywhere But On The Job. This is why I confidently lay claim to a career spanning more breadth, depth, and longevity than anyone else in a worldwide profession I helped create. With a little searching I could illustrate by digging up the 30 years' worth of pocket secretaries I used before the digital era arrived.

This is not a business book. It's a book about life (spoiler: life is difficult). I intend it to be a good read that provides an occasional smile, while always offering useful straight talk about some hard facts (another spoiler: we are all going to die). My credentials are the many decades I spent observing, from a unique vantage point, the way humans interact under stress—and, lately, observing my own behavior in the face of what for the moment let's just call unexpected and permanent stress.

Everyone has a distinct vantage point on life, by the way. Surgeons and lawyers obviously see humanity pass before them in ways only doctors and lawyers can see. The same can be said of teachers and preachers, gas station clerks and bartenders. You all know what doctors and lawyers and teachers and preachers and gas station clerks and bartenders do, so you can imagine their perspective and the kinds of life lessons they learn. Chances are, however, that you have no idea what a readjustment consultant does—let alone how the profession has given me a front-row seat on human nature, complete with backstage pass. I need to brief you on that.

My career as a collection and repo man lasted less than two years. I was able to move up and away from the loan company and into a job in Joan's hometown, Port Huron. I got the job because a priest knew a local bank president. By the way, I also found my first job sailing the Great Lakes by knowing someone. Never let anyone tell you that networking is not the most important grease in the engine of commerce. It is, at every level. Knowing someone is an excellent lubricant to getting in the door as an entry-level hourly wage slave. As a CEO whose company sells a product or service, or as an entrepreneur in almost any field, cultivating a well-earned reputation for being good at what you do is everything. It's an endless concentric circle of people you know and people your representatives know...and a record of good performance...in other words, a network.

When I got in the door at the bank I knew nothing about debt except how to put a tow hitch on a car whose "owner" was 90 days in arrears to the lienholder. But I was forging a unique apprenticeship, a perfect storm of moving to better jobs in a succession that amounted to cross training from every perspective of financial obligation. At the bank I briefly executed personal loans before moving to commercial credit, getting away from my desk and into the shops and offices of customers with operational troubles that had the bank worried about its money. I got a look at retail credit while working for Sears. Then it was on to the heavy-lifting world of industrial credit, where great pyramids of financial obligation are constructed among a company, its bank(s), the company's vendors, and the vendors' banks.

This first decade of my career ashore could not have functioned better as my personal university. The curriculum began with the sad chore of repossessing assets bought with small loans that should not have been made in the first place. On the saddest days of all, a partner and I would enter a home and remove furniture. By the end of my work-for-a-paycheck decade I was assistant credit manager and president of a steel broker's subsidiary whose chief asset was accounts receivable. Almost every day found me analyzing a Paragon Steel customer's debt, proposing a new package of obligations, and striking a restructure agreement. Customers' companies survived because of this work. Paragon Steel itself survived because of this work. Jobs were saved. It felt good. I could now see what the rest of my professional life would look like.

During that first decade I developed the ability to identify the real-world operational problems that lay behind numbers on a shaky balance sheet. I became able to identify what choices—from merely difficult to decisively grim—might lead a company back to financial health or, if no solution was possible, point to how its carcass would be divided among creditors. I became an expert on both the former and the latter. Fortunately the former has always been the goal and, most often, the result.

This no doubt sounds as if I've spent my life in a dull numbers game. Not so. When you see a company's employees on the shop floor, you don't see numbers. You see people depending on a paycheck. Your day instantly becomes anything but dull—especially considering the only way to save anybody's paycheck almost always means eliminating somebody else's paycheck.

When *everybody* has to be sent home, the trauma is exponential, palpable, dramatic. I am the guy in the news stories standing up there delivering the bad news. It's a psychic jolt even to me, even after countless stagings of this drama. I'm not the cause of the layoffs. I'm merely reality's messenger, delivering financial truth first to the client and then to employees. The fact that businesses, like people, have life cycles is just one example of the world looking much different when viewed on the ground rather than in a textbook. One clear example: Years after I moved on and founded my own company, the downsized reality of an evolving steel industry swallowed Paragon Steel—the very place my career discovered its sea legs.

During the last half of my decade as a payroll employee I free-lanced on the side, driven by the all-American motivator of a growing family, new mouths to feed, the need for a bigger house. I consulted for car dealers and retailers and auto parts suppliers and medical clinics, bringing their operations and expenses (including debt) into balance. Between the free-lancing and the day jobs, I built the formidable relationships among businesses, vendors, and their creditors that led to founding McTevia & Associates. While the phrase "troubled company" gained currency as the preferred euphemism for companies choking on debt, I consulted for them, trimming operations and restructuring debt. My business card in those days simply said: "Management and Adjustment Consultants." What got adjusted was debt.

Everyone on the scene in those first years agreed that the young ex-sailor and ex-repo man was a pathfinder, one of a handful defining a profession that became known as "turnaround management." By 1987 enough practitioners were using that term on business cards to form the Turnaround Management Association. Today's worldwide TMA members list degrees and other distinguished abbreviations after their names. I stayed too busy acquiring clients to acquire any sheepskin suitable for framing.

Bankruptcy judges watched my work and began seeking me out to take on cases as a receiver and, years later under new bankruptcy laws, as a trustee. Over the years I've guided scores of cases through Bankruptcy Court. Some companies wind up there because of nefarious greed, MultiVest being a notable example. I took a supermarket chain through bankruptcy after the grocer was found to be overpaying for inventory it bought from itself via hidden ownership. Most insolvent companies however, don't file bankruptcy as a result of prosecution.

The traditional bankruptcy candidate is a company choking on debt, gasping for oxygen while uneasy bankers and vendors tighten the noose because of slow payment or non-payment. An endless list of reasons and excuses can trigger this critical mass—an overoptimistic business plan, or too much generosity by creditors, or a company's own over-generosity in rewarding principals or shareholders, or the arrival of a very large and efficient competitor, or obsolescence in their market, or simple bad luck. For whatever reason, the debt load becomes so heavy that this train which left the station amid so much optimism is grinding toward a slow, sad halt.

On a parallel track, the first goal of my consultancy always has been to *avoid* Bankruptcy Court, a dismal and dismaying place no one wants to be. I saw too many companies get liquidated when they could have survived, at least in some more modest form. Too many creditors and vendors took too much of a haircut. Almost no one was pleased by the outcome. Resolving more cases without filing bankruptcy was the great evolution as turnaround management took shape.

The game-changing process was simple, rooted in my earliest consulting experience. The "out of court settlement" is self-explanatory. It means resolving an unsustainable web of financial obligations with a renegotiated debt structure seeking the best possible and practical outcome for all. That's the carrot. Avoiding the black hole of Bankruptcy Court is the stick.

Having been to this dance for so many decades in so many roles, my task is to arrive on the scene, analyze the numbers, prepare a settlement proposal, and then sell it with unyielding straight talk and an enormous amount of diplomacy. These days my reputation for doing just that, as equitably and practically as possible, can bring a $10 million case under control with a three-page letter to all the parties citing specifics of what the out of court settlement will accomplish.

And there, succinctly and at no extra charge, you have learned not only my job description but also my most vital professional secrets. I hear you scoffing. You think it's painfully obvious to tell a client: "You have only three options: Reduce expenses, or increase revenues, or do both." You are right. Of *course* it's as obvious as saying the force of gravity will grab you if you step off a cliff. But hammering home this important truth to a client can require days and occasionally weeks, even at a high hourly fee. Top management will resist taking even the first steps out of the hole it has dug, believing their company is somehow immune to fiscal gravity. Principals whose sales are dwarfed by inventory, with no upswing in sight, will deny they must take even one of those three steps you rightly believe are obvious. "Things are about to get better," they'll say. Denial, in other words, is standard equipment in human nature.

Human nature is a prime player in every situation I confront. Thinking that something you want is something you need, for example, generates a lot of my business—probably most of it. You know how the wants/needs toggle works in personal behavior. You also know companies are run by people. So if you envision a business principal who thinks a very expensive second home in the country is a need rather than a want...and if you then envision that same principal thinking an over-leveraged expansion of his business is a need rather than a want...that is not a figment of your imagination. It happens all the time. Mistaking wants for needs is the most direct route toward being in the market for a turnaround manager or a bankruptcy judge.

Defining your self-worth according to your material wealth is not, we are told, human nature. Sociologists report finding cultures in which no one gives a damn how much stuff they accumulate, societies where personal possessions do not define "success." But in our society, pressure to accumulate things comes at you 24/7. A middle-class American is expected to live in a McMansion with a three-car garage while taking two vacations a year far away, traveling by air, and renting a car. The brand name and stitching on a pair of blue jeans carry a price tag that would feed a Third World family for at least half a year. You know this, and

I'm not here to deride anyone for enjoying what we used to call 'the good life." I enjoy it myself. But losing affluence, or merely a big chunk of it, does not mean life is no longer worth living.

Believe it or not, advocating this truth is the hardest part of my consulting work. It's not something I get paid for as a turnaround manager. I am hired to be a numbers guy. I'm very good at it, and take pride in it. But at the end of the day—literally, when I put my head on the pillow—it's not numbers flowing through my mind. My work isn't done in a cubicle with a computer and a spreadsheet, then e-mailed to clients I never meet. The action happens at the intersection where balance sheets and human beings cross paths. I meet and work face to face with a troubled company's principals. If their workforce must be sent home, I am the guy at that podium. The people impacted by the numbers are what linger in my mind, the thing that is impossible to leave at the office.

I've seen a lot of tragedy in this business, all fueled by a misguided definition of success and self-worth. It's not that a business principal's kids having to give up tennis lessons and transfer to a public school is a tragedy, or that the Land Rover and Mercedes are going back to the bank. Tragedy lies in the hard-wired idea that these *things* define someone, and there is no way to face tomorrow without them. If this seems like overwrought philosophizing, let me go straight to two words I think about almost every day—*nine suicides.*

All nine were principals of companies that went far down the dark hole and then engaged my company's services. I might not be aware of similar deaths occurring among extended family, or years after I left the picture. I don't know the possible count among many thousands of workers who lost jobs amid downsizing or liquidation, or the count among those workers' families. If suicide is the ultimate tragedy, and losing a nice car or a nice home is merely a stark inconvenience, then what do we call a divorce... or permanent estrangement all up and down a family tree...or the sudden disappearance of people once thought to be close friends? Medium to small tragedies? My own prep schools were a lake freighter and a repo job, so I don't see surrendering an Ivy League education in favor of the local community college as the end of the world. But some do. Under their roof, it's a tragedy unless someone, or the passage of time, convinces them otherwise.

This human factor is why I enter every workday with an agenda that goes beyond crunching numbers, but this wasn't always so. Don't forget, when I was legally stealing cars on behalf of lien-holders I was only 20 years old. I had no deep concern for the guy who would wake up the next morning without wheels. In my first year or two as a consultant I was too busy figuring out what I was doing, and being delighted that my clients liked what I did, to spend much time philosophizing. Within a few years, though, I was fully grasping the depth of despair that lurks behind a business gone bad. I realized that a very high percentage of people whose assets were lost, or merely being downsized, really did believe their lives were over. Their psyches could use some turnaround help, too.

What evolved in response to all that despair was a highly specialized life-coaching segment I build into every case where the personal lifestyles of a client and family are likely to suffer badly. It's a two-step task—assuring them they'll have to surrender some or all of their expensive toys, but also assuring them they still have reason to live, with dignity, a different kind of life. In recent decades that message has included wisdom adapted from a late good friend, a psychiatrist and best-selling author. Since mid-2017 my message sometimes includes the story of a challenge I will be living with for the rest of my own life's journey. From every direction my experience allows, I urge clients not to parlay mere adversity into tragedy. I do whatever I can to help. My work with numbers generates a well-earned income, but I get more satisfaction—more and more so as the years pass—from this other side of my job.

When MultiVest popped onto my plate in 1990, I was well along this value-added path in my consulting business, but we never stop learning, do we? And so it was that a class in the School of Important Things You Can't Learn Anywhere But on the Job was called into session shortly after 5 p.m. in a Miami parking lot.

The attendant spoke first in broken English, nodding his head to indicate the $20 bill I had tossed somewhere on the ground beneath us. He said: "If you think I am going to pick that up, you are wrong. Because I am a person too."

Let's not gild the lily here. No lightning bolt told me I should transfer my allegiance from the Mayo Clinic to the Mother Teresa Calcutta Medical Center. I did not cancel appointments with major clients and rush to the nearest church for confession. I did not rocket into some new sociopolitical orientation (this one was easy, because I have no politics). But let's also not pretend I wasn't shocked by this man's directness, moved by his honesty, and shamed by my behavior. I *was* shocked, moved, and shamed. Profoundly, unforgettably so.

I looked to make sure no one was behind me, backed up the Town Car, found the $20 bill I had tossed at this man for no reason except being in a hurry and being pissed off by a parking fee he had nothing to do with. I picked up the twenty, handed it to him, apologized, and thanked him for the life lesson. I wish I could remember the words I used, but the embarrassment of my actions overrides memory three decades later.

I drove out of the lot and hustled off to my appointment. I was still a hotshot in the middle of a multimillion-dollar story worthy of the news media gaggle awaiting me. But I was wiser than I had been when I got out of bed that morning. Every day is a teacher, if we let it teach.

3

LIKE A THIEF IN THE NIGHT

After first pretending the bad news did not exist, I slowly began confronting it.

⟡

I CAN'T SAY EXACTLY WHERE AND WHEN MY BODY, without my permission, began trying to surrender itself. I can't even cite with certainty the moment I should have noticed it happening.

One day at Nub's Nob ski resort, for example, I decided my downhill days were over, even on the easiest slope. My thigh muscles refused to steer except with enormous and unreliable effort. But I was 75 years old. How many people ski at 75? So I wrote off my unsteadiness to old age. Working in our woods that same year at Highlandview Farms, next door to Nub's Nob, retrospect tells me I probably felt weaker while clearing fallen brush and limbs from hiking trails. That also was no big surprise for a guy headed to the 80 side of 70. Whatever might or might not be creeping up on me, I regarded it as entirely normal, if I even thought about it.

Joan and I created Highlandview Farms in northern Michigan when the grandkids were getting old enough to knock around outdoors. We owned a summer home just down the road from the 20 acres we chose for Highlandview. After we finished developing the farm, Joan settled in to live there year-round. Slowing down my professional life was nothing I was interested in, so I needed to make other arrangements for a world-class commute.

As we began work on the farm in 2007 I had already spent half a century driving back and forth along exurban and suburban Detroit roads and freeways. I was as prepped as one could be for driving 525 miles round trip every weekend to and from Highlandview. Essentially I was trading weekends near the bottom of Lake Huron for weekends near the top of Lake Michigan. I arranged with a Bloomfield Hills hotel to keep a guest room reserved for me near a fitness room and a treadmill. The hotel restaurant came to know my dining schedule and menu tastes intimately. I kept just enough clothes on hand to last a long week. Laundry was automatically picked up unless I was on a business trip or at Highlandview. When I was absent, my wardrobe was moved, by arrangement, to a housekeeping closet so the hotel could rent the room. Not sure how many rooms are rented on indefinite retainer these days, but I spent nine years as an overnight guest at the Kingsley Inn.

We built a new residence on the Highlandview acreage, upgraded an existing riding arena, put in a trout pond, improved a guest cabin, installed numerous amenities. At the end of one hiking trail we built a fire pit for kids and grandkids and called it the S'mores Spot.

Highlandview was bounded by the Huron-Manistee National Forests and Nub's Nob, leaving us without a single neighbor for five miles on our side of the road. The Boyne Highlands ski resort sprawled for several miles to the west. That's two ski resorts within ambitious walking distance. You are guessing correctly that in winter we were buried in fluffy precipitation coming in off nearby Lake Michigan. It was a beautiful, if snowy, setting. What, at this stage of our lives, could possibly better signify sitting on the top of the world than sitting at the top of Michigan's Lower Peninsula at Highlandview Farms?

It doesn't take long for grandchildren to grow up, however. Soon teenaged grandkids were driving themselves up north from metro Detroit, blizzards and all. That was worrisome. And as the S'mores Spot became used less and less, Joan spent more and more time alone in a very large house. Joan and I both had grown up along the St. Clair River, which forms the U.S. border with Canada as it flows from Lake Huron down to Lake St. Clair and then the Grosse Pointes. With my professional success had come our residence in Florida; the house in Harbor Springs; for 25 years a condo in Boothbay Harbor, Maine; and then Highlandview Farms. Great locales one and all, but our genes were stamped "St. Clair River." Joan, alone in the huge farm residence while lifelong friends remained back along the river, was ready to return. Truth be told, I was—substantial dollar loss on a Highlandview sale notwithstanding— more than ready to stop driving an extra 525 miles a week. So in 2015 we moved back beside the St. Clair River to the house where we now live.

We would have made that decision even if I had not meanwhile come to better understand what those hints from my own body were all about. After first pretending the bad news did not exist, I slowly began confronting it.

The day I couldn't make a turn on the ski slope...the sense that in some unmeasured, general way I might be getting weaker—none of this, *none* of it, frightened me in 2012 and into 2013. I was in fact getting older. No big deal. But then something began to happen, incrementally, with my right index finger. I couldn't write very well. I couldn't grip things tightly. Not a *big* deal. But definitely a deal.

In October 2013 when I made my annual trek to Minnesota, I told the Mayo intake physician I was in excellent health except for a touch of weakness as a result of being 76 years old. I said my right index finger—though it gave me no pain at all—was becoming useless, something I attributed to arthritis. Ballpoint pens had developed a mind of their own when I pressed them on paper. I couldn't fasten the top button of a dress shirt. All sorts of gripping tasks were becoming difficult or impossible. I guessed my finger problem had been present and worsening for six months. I told the doctor the regular acupuncture treatments I was getting in Harbor Springs (a relaxation routine I picked up from Joan) seemed to help.

The doctor listened to my symptoms, ignored my self-diagnosis, and scheduled an appointment in the neurology department. The incredibly efficient Mayo Clinic organization chart and infrastructure were about to come through for me. Had I been forced to wander week to week and city to city and facility to facility for the testing and consultation that followed, I might have backed out of the process, useless finger and all.

That first Mayo interaction was on a Wednesday. By Friday all the X-rays and EMGs and blood work had been completed and I sat in an exam room with a neurologist, Bruce R. Krueger, M.D. He had examined the images and lab work and had measured mobility in my limbs and digits. He told me, in that direct and clinical language we all know as we await the most personal of news, that I had an "active myopathy with an inflammatory component."

Today I could deliver a long speech on that subject. On October 24, 2013, I had no idea what Dr. Krueger was talking about. I knew his next sentence would explain it. But in the micro-instant "myopathy with an inflammatory component" caught my ear, it created a certain amount of incipient dread—though hearing "inflammatory" let me rationalize that maybe this problem could be solved with a tube of heat rub from the corner drugstore. Dr.

Krueger said no. He said I "most likely" had *inclusion body myositis.*

It was impressively professional of Dr. Krueger to go straight to his tentative diagnosis of a rare neuromuscular disease. But he said there was no way of knowing for sure without a muscle biopsy. He told me that—Mayo being Mayo—the clinic could do a biopsy during this same Minnesota visit.

How convenient. And what could be a more obvious decision than saying "yes" to getting a biopsy recommended by a neurologist who has just told you that you probably have an incurable disease? Remember, nothing could be more obvious than when I tell my financial "patients" they need to "cut expenses, increase revenues, or do both." Also remember that denial comes as standard equipment with human nature. There's no other explanation for me giving Mayo Clinic the same kind of lame response I hear from my clients. Sitting amid a critical mass of world-renowned physicians and researchers and caregivers, I said, "Thank you very much, but no." I had a kidney stone removed and went home to Michigan.

Even at my age, I continued to think of myself as immortal. After all, I had pursued a healthy lifestyle for 40 years ever since being told on my first visit to Rochester that my choices were to shape up or die. Ever since then I had let the best doctors in the world poke and prod me once every 12 months. That ought to cover it. Even Mayo Clinic said this inclusion body myositis diagnosis was not definite without a biopsy. I was a busy workaholic who felt OK except for a few problems. Who's to say I wasn't just a 76-year-old guy who looked like a 60-year-old, had a little arthritis, and needed to get a little more sleep? I was as irrational, as human, and as deep into denial as any McTevia & Associates client.

The denial soon eroded. During the 2013-14 winter I didn't merely get tired in the woods at Highlandview. My legs had increasing trouble getting over and around fallen trees as I tidied our hiking trails. I stumbled. I nearly fell, several times, while working with my chainsaw.

Something undeniably was happening to my body. I did not respond with a wake-up-in-the-morning-shaking-in-your-boots fear. It was instead a vague dread that snuck in and out of conscious thought like a thief in the night. Over the holidays and on into spring of 2014 the symptoms gained intensity. My neuromuscular deficits had a random selectivity that was, to use a bad pun, unnerving. Some aspects of my physical being seemed to be coming under full siege. Others remained untouched, with absolutely no sign of a threat. The collar-button problem, for example, was an unbearably frustrating affront that met me at the top of every day.

Here was a guy who this afternoon might be deciding how to distribute millions of dollars in contested assets...or counseling how a family business now into its third generation might survive by downsizing and swallowing some pride...a guy perfectly capable of driving to the venue where he will dispense this wisdom...*but a guy who cannot button his shirt.*

Humbling? Yes. Worse yet, after the truth began to seep in, it was borderline frightening, at least in moments I let it be so. It was my 75th Christmas, and opening a greeting card's envelope began to be a challenge. The restaurant packets of jam and jelly I enjoy on my morning toast became at last impossible.

Work, always an effective distraction, remained my conscious priority every day. Subconsciously I was sorting undiminished physical strengths into one pile and emerging physical weaknesses into another. I coped through the spring, reading a bit about IBM (the obvious if at first distracting acronym for inclusion body myositis) while always keeping in mind that no final diagnosis had been rendered. Then, at last, I arranged for Mayo Clinic to do the biopsy I had rejected in October. I remained a fully functioning business professional. Everything was as before—except for this disease, whatever it was. That was the amazing two-sidedness of it all. On the one hand, I maintained an undiminished workaholic caseload. On the other hand, I was beginning to feel shaky while negotiating stairs.

In mid-July 2014 I went up to Rochester and let a Mayo doctor take a muscle tissue sample for biopsy. The clinic's agenda was to diagnose and treat. My agenda was to let Mayo Clinic discover it was all wrong about inclusion body myositis and Jim McTevia. Then the doctors could get on with finding a diagnosis more to my liking, one that wouldn't require me to confront dread head-on.

The July trip was only for the biopsy. My annual physical was not scheduled for three months. So once again I returned home without an official diagnosis. In a day or two I could have gone online and checked the biopsy result. I could have talked to a neurologist about what it meant. Clinic records show a call inviting that kind of interaction was left on my voice mail. If I heard it, I don't remember. I was content instead to bury myself in work, sneak a look at whatever online research I could find about this *possible* diagnosis, IBM, and wait for a face-to-face discussion during my return visit in October.

Human nature, denial, distraction, and the waiting game can never prevail, however. I was about to have not a mere teachable moment, but a remainder-of-your-life lesson.

4

IF IT WALKS LIKE MYOSITIS AND TALKS LIKE MYOSITIS...

*I was in fact getting older.
No big deal. But then something
began to happen, incrementally...*

I DIDN'T HAVE TO WAIT LONG before my year of ducking and denying and worrying and waffling crashed head-on into reality. Did I really spend a whole year side-stepping the truth? Yes. During my 2013 annual exam Dr. Krueger said I "probably" had inclusion body myositis. Nine months later I submitted to a muscle biopsy but made no effort to find out what it revealed. The symptoms, after all, were minor. More or less. Meanwhile, I kept surfing the web and reading about this rare, incurable disease.

If it was incurable, what was the rush? My annual exam was right around the corner. Then I would have no choice but to make peace with the hard truth. That was soon enough for me.

In October 2014, Mayo Clinic scheduled a 1 p.m. neurology appointment for the very first day of my annual visit. Otherwise I would have avoided the reckoning another day or two while my heart, lungs, vision, and liver were tested. Mayo chose the perfect messenger to grab my attention and keep it. Dr. Margherita Milone, M.D, is a renowned neurologist and researcher specializing in muscular diseases, several of which are, unlike inclusion body myositis, household names—ALS (Lou Gehrig's disease), muscular dystrophy, and myasthenia gravis. Besides her clinical and academic credentials, Dr. Milone knows how not to pull punches while delivering a harsh diagnosis.

I sat across from her at her desk. She spoke clearly and articulately, choosing words anyone would understand, putting medical terms into context that defined them. A large desktop computer screen displayed facts related to her message. She was a foremost expert with a biopsy report in hand. I was cornered, finally, with nowhere to run.

I can't quote Dr. Milone's exact words, but

I can tell you she indelibly convinced me that, yes, I had an incurable, progressive muscular disease and that no one knows very much about it.

Attention grabbed.

Attention kept.

Denial ended.

Life changed.

If the speed of light is too fast to comprehend, the speed of thought sometimes seems even faster. So it went with the questions racing through my mind as Dr. Milone filled in the blanks. Most things she was telling me were things I already knew, having given myself an entire year to Google "inclusion body myositis." As she spoke, I checked each fact off an imaginary list while my mind wildly pondered what my future reality might be.

It's usually not hereditary. Check. (Will I be walking into this clinic next year, or will I be in a wheelchair?)

The non-hereditary type, which you have, is called "sporadic" inclusion body myositis, or sIBM. Check. (Having always imagined myself immortal, or having not concerned myself with that issue, and not having socked away enough money to live forever in the manner to which Joan and I had been accustomed—am I going to be able to keep making a living?)

IBM usually strikes after age 50. Check. (And I am considerably past 50. Maybe that's good? Maybe that's bad? Probably doesn't mean a thing.)

Progressive weakness of legs, arms, fingers, and wrists is typical. Check. (Again—will I be in a wheelchair next year? Or will that happen next month? Or 10 years from now?)

Symptoms vary, and so does the rate at which the disease progresses. Check. (No one knows much at all about IBM!)

Dr. Milone didn't use the word "terminal," but I had no doubt—as I had been subconsciously convincing myself for a while—that unless run over by a truck or infected with some exotic fatal virus or felled by an unexpected massive heart attack or done in by a gun-toting felon... then this thing that won't let me button my shirt is what will one day kill me.

My layman's knowledge might have set a world's record for a patient entering a diagnosis consultation. For sure no one ever compiled so much self-learning about a disease while devoting so much time to pretending or at least hoping there was no reason to know anything about it. Now, with all diagnostic doubt dismissed by Dr. Milone, I was terrified by what she was telling me. Wherever fear popped up, my mind ran over and knocked it down like smoke jumpers controlling a wildfire. It mostly worked. I had been delivered the unadulterated truth and would have to live with it. It's not as if I had been blind-sided, not now. I had been warned about this freight train. I was ready.

Dr. Milone said there were "anecdotal reports" of temporary improvement or slowed IBM progression among patients who underwent immunotherapy with the drug methotrexate. If that interested me, it would require a succession of treatments and would be delivered by a medical facility back in Michigan. Interested? Me? You bet.

I thanked Dr. Milone, then completed my annual battery of tests and exams. I left Rochester after a visit that was, obviously, a benchmark for my forthcoming battle with IBM—a disease that is all about benchmarks. Every case is a little different, occasionally a lot different. Inclusion body myositis is rare enough, and only recently studied enough, that no huge body of knowledge exists about its course across human lifetimes. Because it's not curable, the main reason for my future clinic visits would simply be to measure deficits and compare them with previous visits. The benchmarks of my strength and mobility would be headed downward. So I thought of each upcoming visit as the opposite of those marks on the wall where parents measure their kids' increasing height. In that sense, October 2014 at Mayo Clinic was the prime benchmark in another sense, the time and place where reality replaced denial.

If methotrexate treatments might slow that downward curve even a little, I was all for giving it a try. I fully understood it would be an experiment in which I was the test tube, and serious side effects were possible. Hey, it might work. Sign me up. In January 2015 I was administered two doses of the stuff in Michigan. In February, a couple days after the second dose, Joan and I flew down to our place in Florida and I almost died.

Being aboard a commercial airplane is a good place to pick up whatever virus might be prevalent at the moment. Having also just completed my second methotrexate treatment must have created a perfect incubator for whatever made me violently ill the day after we landed. I became extraordinarily sick with flu symptoms and was carted off to Jupiter Medical Center with bronchial pneumonia and severely diminished lung capacity. My immune capacity had plunged, which roughly translates to methotrexate poisoning. I was a very sick 78-year-old puppy. They kept me on oxygen for a week, and—in an era when pushing the patient out the door as soon as possible is the goal—kept me hospitalized for two more weeks. I almost beat IBM the hard way. I had no serious quarrel with that. I knew the methotrexate presented risks.

There were other lessons learned in the Jupiter hospital, however.

After my lung capacity returned to normal, the pulmonologist who had been working my case pulled up a chair one day and began going over the list of medications on my chart.

He noted I had been taking Allopurinol for almost four decades.

"Do you have gout?"

"No, but I had it 35 years ago."

"Well, you don't have it now. I insist you stop taking Allopurinol."

Losing Allopurinol would be like losing an old friend. In ancient times few people lived as long as I had been ingesting this gout drug. To this day I can remember the excruciating pain I felt in a toe, by far the strongest pain I ever have endured, and the trip to an emergency room where I made Allopurinol's acquaintance. But 40 years of a healthy lifestyle had my uric acid down. Bye-bye, Allopurinol.

And I could see where the pulmonologist was heading.

Toprol. Same deal. I no longer had a blood pressure problem. I was being told to discontinue Toprol.

And another drug, one that would become an interesting and contentious footnote in my quest to hold IBM at bay while juggling expert advice and my common-sense judgment. Lipitor is a leading member of the drug group known as statins. They are primarily used to lower cholesterol levels. Some users associate statins with weight loss. I had been taking Lipitor ever since that day Mayo Clinic saved my life by scaring me into pursuing a lifestyle designed to keep my body going, rather than a path certain of putting me in an early grave. I no longer had a cholesterol problem.

"Statins," my pulmonologist insisted, "are a leading cause of muscle problems. And you don't need statins."

Furthermore, I said loudly to myself, a muscle disease is killing me, and I would rather that happen later than sooner. I needed no persuasion to yank statins of any kind from my med regimen.

Let's sort this out and be clear about it. I am

not a physician. I am not a pharmacist. I am just a health-care consumer and citizen who—like millions of other citizens—thinks we are an overmedicated society. Back when I was a flabby 40 years old in awful health, I was prescribed, and began taking, certain medications that helped counter a self-destructive lifestyle. Not just the high cholesterol and blood pressure, but even the gout was lifestyle-related. I had turned my lifestyle around. I ran all those 10Ks, then became a treadmill maniac for whatever duration this body could handle it. But as decades passed, I was still taking these medications. A Florida doctor I had never seen before told me to dump them. I probably could have gone to another doctor down the street, or even elsewhere in the same hospital, and gotten a different opinion, or have been told, "it's your choice." But this pulmonologist's advice reeked of common sense. It wasn't coming from a tabloid newspaper. He had, after all, overseen my recovery from a very bad situation.

I made a health-care consumer's decision to remove the three meds and, of course, to keep monitoring my cholesterol, blood pressure, and uric acid. When my blood pressure and uric acid level began to climb again, I returned to recommended doses of Toprol and Allopurinol. I'm still off statins, and expect to remain off them the rest of my life. This was my choice amid a unique set of circumstances. It is *not* specific advice for anyone else's medicine cabinet, just a little advocacy for giving lifestyle a chance to prevail. The bottom line is that if I had lived my first 40 years the way I lived my second 40 years, I probably would not have been taking any of these meds in the first place.

I dived back into the business world. I hadn't left it, really. Never have. But you do ease up a bit when your quarterly report includes an eventful trip to Mayo, the Thanksgiving and Christmas holidays, a couple rounds of immunotherapy, and almost a month lying in a hospital bed. Not a good winter.

How about the IBM benchmarks? Now that I had survived the methotrexate, I was stable again. Clients weren't likely to notice my symptoms. I did not risk stairs in public. In private I grasped stairway railings and walls tightly, lifting my legs warily from one step to the next. Smartphones and laptops meant no one saw me struggle with a ballpoint. When your fingers are fully functional, typing a grocery list on a tiny smartphone keyboard might seem more difficult than writing with a pen. With IBM, it's the opposite, a part of that bizarre all-day toggle among functions that work just as well as when you were 21 and other functions that are deteriorating badly. The muscle groups first attacked by myositis—in the thighs and fingers—set me up for abject failure on the ski slope and, before long, prevented me from signing a check by hand. Nonetheless, for some unknown period of time (many years, I hoped), myositis would have no meaningful impact on my work. That's the way I attacked the rest of 2015.

I've been honest here about the waffling, and the denial, and the delay, and the unstated fear leading up to this point. I'm also being honest when I tell you there was never any question that, once cornered, I would fight. I wasted a day or two feeling sorry for myself after my meeting with Dr. Milone, but then my battle with IBM began in earnest. Not a dumb, futile struggle to achieve the impossible, but a battle fought with great and growing clarity.

Most basically I began to comprehend that not only was I not immortal, but I probably had lived more years than the number of years remaining for me. Someone making a good living as a numbers guy understands he won't live to be 156 years old. But we're talking psychology, not arithmetic. If you don't look at the hourglass, you don't see how time has drained away.

If you stay too busy to dwell on how many calendars you've burned through, that's not entirely a bad thing. If sporadic inclusion body myositis hadn't started atrophying my muscles, would I *ever* have noticed the dwindling time I had left on my clock? Of course. We all have markers we can't ignore. My mother died just 15 months after Dr. Milone confirmed the IBM diagnosis. Marie McTevia was 100 years old. She had a good long run. I was already 79 when she passed.

We had left Highlandview Farms and moved back south to our current house on the St. Clair River. I was commuting to a northern Detroit suburb, working full-time as a consultant—to use the more up-to-date euphemism—to *companies in transition*. In that sense, you could say not much had changed in 60 years except my long-term goals and reasonable expectations. In another sense, I had embarked upon the greatest challenge and most spiritual years of my life.

5

STARING UP AT MURPHY

*I was treading water in an unlikely trough
between a career that was sailing smooth seas
under pleasant skies, and a health situation
growing ominously darker.*

❧

I DID NOT SLIP BACK INTO DENIAL.

Do not get me wrong on this. I didn't.

Not exactly.

Human nature is so hard-wired toward rejecting bad news, or ignoring it, or at least trying to work around it that whenever possible we find ways of, let's say, not denying but *forgetting* adversity, major or minor. One method is to stay busy. And as you know, I am as good as it gets at staying busy.

In the spring of 2015 I was serving on six

boards of directors and dealing with four major new clients whose operations reached coast to coast. In other words, I was as busy as ever. IBM diagnosis notwithstanding, I loved every minute of being busy, as always. Those three medically miserable weeks in a Florida hospital passed quickly from the rear-view mirror as the year revved up. I was on my game, right where I have always wanted to be.

My professional life morphed into a less-is-more profile when, in my mid-70s, I began downsizing McTevia & Associates. Instead of a battalion of full-time associates, the company at this writing has become basically me, an office staff, and whatever number of specialists I might need to contract on a case-by-case basis. During the intentional shrinkage in number of clients, I began doing a larger percentage of the hands-on work myself. Today my personal income is not appreciably different than when I had dozens of employees to keep busy and to manage. So I was in a very good place professionally as I emerged from that bad bout of methotrexate therapy.

On the health side of the ledger, when I trekked to Rochester in October 2015 it was almost as if even the medical profession was trying to divert my attention from myositis. Not really, of course. My IBM hadn't gone away and never would. I displayed no significant worsening in muscular benchmarks, however, and seemed to be functioning in daily life about as well as I had been a year earlier. The imperative clinical message this time became: Listen up, you have another problem that might kill you—no, *probably* will kill you—before IBM kills you. I suddenly had a brand-new disease to go into denial about.

Even if sleep apnea has not struck within your family or circle of friends, you probably know the basics. Apnea makes you stop breathing for abnormal, prolonged periods while you sleep. This is not good. A fatal heart attack can result. And here I was at the Mayo Clinic, where I once was told I probably had IBM but would need a biopsy to know for sure, but told them— the first time around—no thanks, I'm not going to do that. Now I was being told I probably had sleep apnea, and Mayo had a sleep disorders center right down the hall and around the corner. *I should get tested for sleep apnea on this very visit.*

You know how that went.

I was feeling good...well, I did have those troubling onset IBM symptoms, but they could be called minimal. Sleep problems? You're kidding. Great sleep has always come natural to me, even more so after I began living a healthy lifestyle. I got eight or ten hours of shut-eye a night. Mayo wanted me to go spend a night sleeping while wired-up to prove that, in fact, I put my life at risk every time I lay my head on a pillow? "No thanks. I'm returning to Michigan and getting back to being busy and making a living." You have to admire my honesty in telling you such things, if not my refusal to hear the best doctors' best advice.

It's astounding, in retrospect, to count up how long this game of Let's Pretend Everything Is OK continued. My mother's death in January 2016 gave me one more reminder that, yeah, I will probably die someday. But that year I took on two additional directorships, several major new clients, and numerous lecture engagements. I keep telling you I was busier than ever, but it's true. By October 2016 it was Yogi's "déjà vu all over again"—back to Rochester for the annual Mayo exam and to hear old news: I still had IBM, but sleep apnea was likely to kill me first. No doubt I was in denial regarding sleep disorder. But I honestly believed I was snoozing like an infant Rip Van Winkle. So I skipped the testing, went back home, and two months later added a major multi-state client to my existing workload.

That takes us to 2017, and that is where the shabby fabric of my medical fantasy began to unravel.

The year began well enough. I took on a client with a presence in three Upper Midwest states. I was traveling a lot in the Piper Navajo that I have been using in my business for many years. Clients and directorships had me constantly on the go. The directorships had become an important part of my life. Federal oversight left corporations with no choice but to appoint board members who possessed expertise, pay them meaningfully, and expect board members in return to do meaningful due diligence on corporate affairs. Whenever flying in the Navajo I had come to need a hand climbing aboard, but no big deal. My physical limitations were manageable. The apnea was something I simply paid no attention to. Couldn't see it, couldn't feel it, not a single clue of anything to worry about. Why bother?

But one day IBM gave me not a clue or a premonition but a punch to the gut regarding what this disease has in mind for me.

I was strolling with Murphy, my black 6-year-old Scottish terrier. He and I have taken hundreds of walks in Michigan and, as on this day, in Jupiter, Florida. It was a beautiful day, the essence of why people who love their native Michigan nonetheless can't resist, come February, waking up 1,300 miles south in Florida. Joan and I had traded Boca Raton for a Jupiter community where curving lanes wrap around homes with pools and well-kept grounds. It's as pleasant a haven as you will find for walking in a T-shirt and shorts. On this day Murphy and I were enjoying it immensely.

Here's the thing about what happens when sporadic inclusion body myositis causes a fall. You are walking, or merely standing and preparing to take a step, and the mechanism your body uses to control and propel your leg bones—the thigh muscles...quadriceps and hamstrings—suddenly are simply *not there*. The seamlessness of what happens is the most frightening part. It happens so fast it seems not that the muscles relinquish control, but that they never had it. And you are going down to the ground, and you are landing at least double speed because you don't have that millisecond warning that the fall has begun, so you're halfway down before you realize it. Before you can have even a lightning-quick thought about the process, IBM puts your body on the ground. And steals your normalcy.

Murphy was confused. I was several things.

My knees and elbows were bloody. I was embarrassed. And I was scared. And then I was embarrassed some more. What in the world does embarrassment have to do with such things? I mean, it wasn't about stumbling gracelessly. I wasn't drunk. I went to the pavement because my body refused, unexpectedly and instantly, to do basic things that bodies do. All because of a rare, debilitating, incurable disease—and I am feeling *embarrassed*? Human nature again. It makes no sense that I would feel such profound humiliation. But we all hunger to keep up with the pack, to avoid suggesting we might not be able to do so—even if we have valuable skills, even though the pack should not care that we are not *normal*. How many millions of human beings across the centuries have been *embarrassed* by an inability to keep up even as they drew their last breath? We all want to function normally, to be *busy* across every moment of our timeline. Especially if we turn out not to be immortal after all. So never discount the importance of embarrassment in the life of anyone who fears not being able to keep up, which I suspect describes the majority of mankind.

I got up. Murphy and I made our way back to the house. I washed off the blood and tended to the scrapes. This was entirely new turf for me. It had been three years and four months since Dr. Krueger told me I probably had IBM, two years and four months since the biopsy confirmed it, one year and four months since the sleep apnea card was played onto the table. And after all that medical advice, I had reached my best understanding of reality not while talking to a white-coated professional reeking of expertise, but while lying on the pavement looking up at a Scottish terrier who couldn't tell me what the hell had just happened.

I knew the answer, of course. But I wanted to step beyond embarrassment and fear and, despite the prospect of future bloodied knees and elbows, get on with my normal life. I needed to keep up. I insisted on it, even though for the first time in my life I was dealing with something I didn't know how to conquer and couldn't learn how to conquer.

That winter and spring I fell several more times, in Florida and in Michigan. But 2017 nonetheless accelerated along both trajectories of my life—professionally and as an IBM case (there really should be a better word than "victim" or "sufferer," or even "patient"). My consultancy caseload and directorships did not decline. Nor, for the first half of the year, did

IBM's signals of future bad news diminish. My focus shifted a bit, away from hiding the disease from myself and toward hiding it from others. Surprisingly, it wasn't difficult.

It wasn't as if I couldn't walk (though I avoided public stairways and inclines if they lacked railings). It wasn't as if I went about my business in leg braces or even using a cane (keep in mind the United States president was infinitely more incapacitated while fighting World War II but, thanks to cooperative news media, no one noticed). For me, avoiding any appearance of having a muscular disease was much more subtle. I was slightly surprised and enormously gratified, for example, to discover that prospective clients didn't seem to care that I quit wearing neckties and wore a sweater over a shirt, leaving that pesky top button unbuttoned.

In my professional life, in fact, IBM did not arise as an issue in 2017. Not at all. I never talked about it in business chatter. I still don't. This hasn't been conscious avoidance but simply that my professional style is to be cordial (unless circumstances dictate otherwise), perhaps tell a joke (usually one good enough to draw an unforced laugh), then get down to business without small talk. Someday I might be in a wheelchair, in which case I still plan to be a full-time professional. I imagine the subject of why I am able to sail across the room so quickly will come up then.

Pure luck also helped me keep IBM out of any client's thoughts as 2017 passed while I came to fully understand this disease. That is, I never once fell or even staggered badly in the presence of a client. In fact—you can hear me knocking loudly on wood—at this writing I have only fallen once in the presence of any confidant and once in the company of strangers. The confidant was Murphy, who didn't seem to care as long as I got back up and walked him home. The strangers were other passengers in a busy airport concourse as I rushed to catch a flight. The onlookers were neither clients nor friends, and most were in too big a hurry to pay much attention. I was nevertheless profoundly embarrassed.

Despite being born the year the Queen Mary sailed on her maiden voyage (a fact, not a typo), I've never resisted technological progress. Digital gadgets, home theaters, the breathtaking communication revolution launched by the Internet—all have been my friends from their beginnings. Decades before the cellphone was invented, I had a Ma Bell "mobile phone" in my car. Those things were not really phones, but radio devices that allowed you to contact a Ma Bell operator who also had a radio and who then patched you into your phone call. It was like a Dick Tracy wrist radio, except that if you strapped the device on your wrist you would break your arm. In my years as a young professional I loved to get on a boat and leave the shore behind. My business demanded staying in touch frequently, though, and I seldom ventured more than half an hour from the nearest dock that boasted a payphone.

I was an enthusiastic early user of the Internet even though it did not become a commercial reality until after I was well past eligibility age for AARP membership. In the summer of 2017, back home in Michigan and at age 80 prodded by my new medical realities, I doubled-down on web surfing in search of every known fact about sporadic inclusion body myositis—or at least those facts that a mere turnaround manager could understand. All this self-education would have happened as a matter of course, but I had plenty of outside inspiration...such as when an adult granddaughter—an M.D. specializing in neurology (life is filled with amazing coincidences)—visited and asked why I was wearing, on a beautiful weekend day, clothing that covered my legs and elbows.

I was treading water in an unlikely trough between a career that was sailing smooth seas under pleasant skies, and a health situation growing ominously darker. It's difficult to believe how much good came back at me from the thousands of clicks I made among the dot.coms and dot.orgs, from link to link, from shared experience to shared experience.

In one case, the search led me to the obituary of an old family friend a few miles up the river from our home in St. Clair. He had died while suffering a debilitating disease, as had his father. Yes, some of life's coincidences are so amazing as to defy belief. Both my friend and his father had myositis. I had been aware they had a rare muscular disease. Details such as the disease's complicated, seldom-heard name seemed, at the time, irrelevant to me. It's likely father and son had a type of IBM even more rare than mine—the same disease, but passed from one generation to the next. My more common rare disease (wrap your mind around that one) appears in a family tree unexpectedly and unannounced. That's why it's technically known as *sporadic* inclusion body myositis, or sIBM.

Several articles I found on the Internet reported instances of acupuncture providing some level of temporary IBM symptom relief. That's what the methotrexate therapy was intended to provide, and you know how that turned out. Acupuncture, though, is something I was familiar with—not as IBM therapy but as a first-class source of relaxation and stress relief. When we moved back south from Highlandview Farms, I had not gotten around to finding a new acupuncturist, and thought nothing of it. By chance, after reading about acupuncture and IBM, I learned that an M.D. for whom Joan worked years ago, and since then a lifelong social friend, had a son who recently had completed three years of study in Chinese medicine and acupuncture. "Bingo!" I didn't realize how big a "bingo!" this would be, but I began getting regular acupuncture from a young practitioner named Jason Go.

I also stumbled upon a southwest Michigan newspaper article about a man named Jim Mathews, a pharmacist and businessman of considerable success, someone else who—despite taking care of his body—had wound up with this unfamiliar muscle disease that afflicts perhaps 20,000 Americans, almost all of whose muscles will deteriorate and continue to atrophy after leaving them in a wheelchair. How many things might I relate to while reading a profile of Jim Mathews?

Beyond that, Jim is a member of the Myositis Association, a nationwide group of myositis patients known to its members as TMA. If you have an excellent memory you will recall that the Turnaround Management Association is also known as the TMA. I've never been a joiner, never even signing up with the association for members of the profession I helped invent. But I promptly joined this other TMA, eagerly exchanged e-mails with Jim Mathews, and arranged a lunch meeting. Jim is a bright, articulate man who works hard to build networks among fellow IBM patients. He is a member of the TMA national board. Jim and I communicate regularly about our shared experiences and we trade articles to be read. I would be more active in TMA (myositis version) if I were not so busy doing things members of the other TMA (Turnaround Management Association) do. Would our contact have occurred without the Internet? Maybe. But it might have taken a year or two instead of a day or two.

I found and read hundreds of articles and web posts about IBM. Some were strongly academic, some were written by academics for public consumption, some were simplified "pop" pieces written by authors of unknown qualifications. The sheer volume of material was somehow reassuring. Clearly, I was not alone.

Reading everything you can get your hands on regarding the facts of a topic means standing beside a great revolving and redundant circle—like a baggage carousel—from which new nuggets of information appear and demand to be grabbed. Spend enough time poring over material and you soon accumulate a good layman's understanding of the things that most obviously concern you—is this really going to kill me, and when, and how, and what will everyday life be like along that path, and what can I do about traveling that path in the best possible way? And where do I go to make sure I get the best possible professional advice and therapy? In short, who knows the most about these things...and what do I do to become his or her patient?

Every time I stepped away from this carousel of information at the end of a surfing session, I found the compass pointed to Baltimore, a city that had never figured in my life, and to Johns Hopkins University's Myositis Center, the top of the line among facilities studying and treating myositis. This wonderful thing called the Internet allowed me to drill a little deeper merely by punching keys at my desk in St.

Clair. That's how I was able to decide that of all the doctors in the world, I wanted Tom Lloyd, Ph.D. and M.D., to examine my case.

You cannot imagine my upbeat frame of mind and my confidence, only weeks after wearing shirts and pants to cover the cuts and bruises I sustained while falling. By God, I would go out east and show these myositis experts that an 80-year-old man working full-time in a high-pressure job might just be their first opportunity to observe this disease traveling a different path.

That no doubt sounds stranger than strange, a bit crazy even. But the fact is this. After returning to acupuncture treatments on June 23, a marvelous thing had happened. I stopped falling.

6

A PILGRIMAGE TO BALTIMORE

*When heading into battle it's instinctual,
useful, and in some ways even comforting
to know your enemy, to have all the
knowledge you can find.*

❧

THINK OF ALL THOSE ONE-PANEL CARTOONS where a pilgrim has climbed a mountain seeking a cave-dwelling guru who will reveal the secret of life. The guru's wisdom always turns out to be nothing more than a punch line. Guru cartoons are an amusing take on the eternal search for knowledge, expertise, and—this is where our old friend human nature takes the quest over the top—magical solutions. I was not pursuing quixotic quests in 2017. I knew science had not found a miracle cure for inclusion body myositis and would not find one in a week or two. But I was determined to find a figurative mountain where a foremost community of real-world myositis gurus devoted themselves to studying the science of my muscle disease. I would climb up there, get the benefit of their expertise, and increase my understanding of what was going on with my own deteriorating muscles. That was the realistic part of my first trip to Baltimore.

My unrealistic expectations were vague, unstated, mostly subconscious. I must have believed the experts would be stunned when I showed them how well my 80-year-old body was coping with IBM. Why not? I was in fact doing very well in the second half of 2017. I had quit falling. I was as busy as ever. My mind was in a very good place. I looked forward to this medical pilgrimage with no trepidation. I didn't expect the unexpectable. But in retrospect, it's clear that deep down my attitude was that, working together, the experts and I would *handle my problem.*

I had no specific idea what "handle my problem" meant. No doubt my inner self believed that going into full-bore attack mode would reveal *something*—not a miracle but a therapy, a medication, a regimen, patient education and training, whatever—that would let me coexist with a debilitating disease while, by the way, pursuing my profession exactly as I had for more than half a century. I could not beat inclusion body myositis into submission. But no way was I going to overlook any opportunity to punch back. I might even stagger my foe for a round or two.

It had been a good year for self-directed study, scouring the Internet, meeting Jim Mathews, learning about (and from) the Myositis Association, poring over pamphlets and articles. Evenings spent swiping my iPad screen in pursuit of medical knowledge made me wonder how Abe Lincoln managed to teach himself law while reading books by candlelight. I wasn't as good a student as Abe Lincoln, but Abe couldn't possibly have been more eager for the task. When I read about IBM attacking the thigh muscles, it wasn't theoretical. I'd look at my legs and think, "Well, you guys, will you keep me on my feet tomorrow? Or when I take Murphy for a walk, will I have another fall?" That's one way of explaining the difference between me and Murphy, who watched in blissful ignorance as I lay sprawled on Florida pavement. I understood exactly what had happened. Murphy is a smart dog, but not that smart. For sure Murphy has no clue of what will be happening in the future. Philosophers have been talking for centuries about who comes out ahead on that particular difference between man and dog.

Ever since the Mayo Clinic biopsy nailed the IBM diagnosis, I've often said, "Unlike most people, I already know what is going to kill me." I still put it that way, though it's technically not true. Mayo Clinic doctors didn't use the word "fatal" when telling me I have an incurable and progressively debilitating disease. Any death certificate that cites inclusion body myositis as cause of death is probably inaccurate. IBM's relationship with mortality does not work that way.

If an IBM patient dies after falling and striking his head on a marble tabletop, head trauma will be the cause of death—not the weakening muscles that caused the fall. Similarly, about half of IBM patients develop dysphagia, or swallowing problems. If someone in an advanced stage of IBM and dysphagia dies after aspirating food or fluids into the lungs, IBM will not technically be the cause of death. This disease attacks and slowly wastes certain skeletal muscles, notably in the upper legs and forearms and often in the throat and face. Bad things happen as a result. But IBM would not be the real cause of death.

That's grim stuff. But it's knowledge. When heading into battle it's instinctual, useful, and in some ways even comforting to know your enemy, to have all the knowledge you can find. Steely, detached, stoic demeanor was therefore not necessary for such heavy reading. I did, and continue to do, my layman's best to understand sporadic inclusion body myositis.

Don't forget, too, that some contracts with fate fall due sooner than others. Consider how my medical enemy relates to time and the calendar. IBM does not end life's journey in a few weeks or months, or even just a couple years. If Mayo Clinic doctors had told me I would not live to see the next Christmas, I doubt I would have wasted precious time seeking details about my disease. But that's not how IBM takes you down.

There's a cosmic roll of the dice in these things. Consider two remarkable bookend diseases, IBM and ALS, which have much in common despite their fundamental differences. At first glance, the two have nothing at all in common except that both waste muscles of the body. Dig a little deeper and one discovers that ALS wastes muscle by attacking nerves and IBM attacks muscle cells directly—meaning they seem to have even less in common. But dig still deeper and the mystery bends back to where muscle and nerve meet...and we find that key parts of what little we understand about IBM are things we have learned from studying ALS.

Most people know at least a little about amyotrophic lateral sclerosis. Lou Gehrig was a national hero, a baseball star so durable he was known as the Iron Horse. When he took himself out of the Yankees lineup in May 1939 because his deteriorating muscles had diminished his skills, Gehrig had played 2,130 consecutive big-league games. He died two years later at age 38. To this day ALS is commonly known as Lou Gehrig's disease. It attacks almost all the body's muscles, including those that allow speaking, swallowing and, ultimately, breathing. Survival after onset typically is just three to five years. The toll on core body musculature, not "merely" on mobility, is terrible. In the normal course of events, death certificates cite ALS as cause.

Inclusion body myositis, on the other hand, attacks fewer, very specific sets of muscles. About 80 percent of IBM cases are diagnosed after age 50. We tend to live a long time after diagnosis. Statistics—as with most knowledge about IBM—remain very much a work in progress. My case will contribute to that statistical work. But it's fair to say most IBM patients who do not die of complications from a fall, or from aspiration pneumonia, might live almost as long as if they had never heard of IBM. Impending departure from this planet is not the compelling issue with IBM. The issue is quality of life.

Not many diseases present you with the foreknowledge of a long, steady decline from normal mobility to using a cane to using a walker to using a wheelchair...from being active to being sedentary...from not being able to button a shirt or wield a ballpoint pen to not being able to get out of a chair without help. During this decline it is not unusual for an IBM patient to live 15 or 20 years despite being diagnosed at an advanced age. The variables of declining ability across time differ from case to case, but the end game is universally not good. It's a daunting prospect for every patient. Until my IBM diagnosis, it would never have occurred to me that living to 100—like my mother and grandmother—might not be something I'd look forward to bragging about.

If I already knew in the fall of 2017 most of what you just read, how can I possibly say my mind was in a good place, and I had no trepidation about submitting myself to examination by experts in an incurable disease I know is going to kill me unless I am first brought down by a car wreck, or a different disease, or, as the insurance actuaries say, an act of God? Or, for that matter, sleep apnea?

Friends and relatives might point to stubbornness. Business associates might point to a steadfast determination to solve the problem at hand. I can't deny those traits. But if a single factor explained my upbeat nature, it was acupuncture.

No, no, no—I do not believe ancient Chinese needle therapy can cure IBM, or even hold it at bay indefinitely. But let me tell you about my experience with Chinese alternative medicine—which is classified as a pseudoscience but is available at the Mayo Clinic's wellness center. That's the way it goes with remedies and therapies that came into play thousands of years before modern medicine. Keep in mind I am a skeptic, by nature and by decades practicing a profession that demands nothing if not vigilant skepticism. Yet not for a moment do I believe my acupuncture experience was a placebo effect.

I was diagnosed with IBM in my late 70s. That isn't, believe it or not, a spectacularly advanced age to get the news. It's generally believed that—because most IBM diagnoses occur from late middle age well into post-retirement age—the first few years of symptoms are commonly dismissed as normal slowing down with passing years. The patient's first fall is typically the first bright red flag. I understand the pattern. But I believe the acupuncture treatments I began merely as relaxation therapy did in fact diminish my early symptoms and are one reason my IBM was not diagnosed sooner. That's purely amateur speculation. You need several platoons of patients, divided into a control group and another group actually receiving acupuncture, to approach the truth, clinically speaking. But consider the following.

Once a year for 40 years one of the world's premier medical facilities took its best shot at finding things wrong with me. When I made the typical IBM-onset complaint of lost finger-flexion and gripping ability, I was diagnosed in Rochester before I ever took a fall. When we moved from Highlandview Farms back to southeast Michigan, I was too busy to find a new acupuncturist and I discontinued needle sessions. I didn't give it much thought. Then, down in Florida (no acupuncture) and back in suburban Detroit (no acupuncture), I began falling.

This is when I sought out Jason Go, my doctor friend's son. Jason is no casual acupuncturist, having spent three years in formal training as a traditional Chinese medicine practitioner. After Jason began treating me I didn't fall again for almost half a year. That came after several family medical emergencies occasioned serious stress, which again led to skipping acupuncture sessions. I immediately fell twice within a few days. I resumed acupuncture—and quit falling (months before these word were written). If that's a placebo, I'll take two, please.

This still proves nothing, of course. I don't pretend that Chinese needles will prevent any of IBM's inevitable end game. I don't play a doctor, not on TV and not even in these pages. I am also not a scientist. But I tried a medical experiment, methotrexate therapy, and it damned near killed me. I tried acupuncture with good results. That's why you can feel free to picture me as the guy on a poster saying, with enthusiasm: "Who knows? But I swear by it. With good reason." So much so that I found another skilled acupuncturist in Florida, Cheryl Sheriff. Now I welcome needle treatment at least twice a week, whether I'm working northern or southern latitudes.

With spirits buoyed by several months of not falling, with a track record of stubbornness, and with a long career as a problem-solver, I quickly found the medical gurus I was looking for. Neurologists at Johns Hopkins University in Baltimore have long been ranked at or near the top of researchers and clinical practitioners in their field. IBM is a muscular disease, not a brain or nerve disease. Scientific inquiry, however, travels along paths of connectivity, as between ALS and IBM, not following preconceived ideas of where truth lies. The biggest reason it didn't take long to find my quest's destination is that the Johns Hopkins Myositis Center is a unique facility dedicated to inflammatory muscle diseases including dermatomyositis, juvenile myositis, polymyositis, and inclusion body myositis.

Don't be confused by the large words and by three diseases that haven't been mentioned here and likely won't be again. All four types of myositis cause inflammation and weakening of various muscles. But those other three types turn at a different fork in the road. They are clearly autoimmune diseases, meaning the immune system attacks the muscle. Women develop the other three more often, whereas IBM is more common in men. And, in a compelling difference from my vantage point, all three of the other myositis types can be treated. Symptoms can be eliminated entirely in some cases.

Only about 50,000 Americans have some form of myositis. Timely and accurate diagnosis of rare diseases with overlapping or similar symptoms—not just across various types of myositis but some other diseases, including muscular dystrophy—cried out for a specialized facility. The JHU Myositis Center drew an immediate and increasing flow of patients from around the country, and the synergy among JHU's researchers and clinicians put the Myositis Center at the cutting edge of myositis research and treatment. As I said, finding my figurative mountain of myositis gurus was not difficult.

I arranged the appointment myself, without a referral from Mayo Clinic. I guess I didn't want to offend or irritate anyone at the iconic facility that had become, for all practical purposes, my primary physician. After four decades of seeking regular medical attention nowhere but Rochester, Minnesota, I don't foresee ever changing that relationship. But as regards the outstanding medical peril staring me in the eye, I wanted the most renowned destination dedicated solely to researching and treating myositis.

I gathered up my Mayo Clinic records, and those from the Jupiter hospital where I spent a month after the methotrexate disaster, and sent them off to Johns Hopkins. I told intake personnel I wanted a second opinion, which is medical talk for "I don't like what nature is doing to me, and no one is performing magic to cure it, so I'm shopping around." I asked if I might have an appointment with a specific practitioner.

That would be Dr. Tom Lloyd, who, after finishing his three-year neurology residency at Johns Hopkins, began a one-year fellowship in neuromuscular diseases at Johns Hopkins in 2007, the very year the Myositis Center was launched. Dr. Lloyd's entire career seems, in retrospect, to have destined him to be out front in the effort to understand and treat inclusion body myositis. Lloyd was still an undergraduate at Rice University in Houston when he became especially interested in how human cells work, a fascination heightened by summer research experiences across the street at the Baylor College of Medicine. As with many physician researchers, he chose a path that earned him both a Ph.D. and an M.D.— thinking scientifically about diseases as well as treating patients struck by those diseases—in a seven- to eight-year program at Baylor.

The Baylor years nurtured young Tom Lloyd's interest in neuromuscular diseases, particularly ALS. As a molecular and cellular biology Ph.D. he studied the science of how motor neurons—the nerve cells that control muscles—function. In other words, Dr. Lloyd was immersed early on in seeking to understand how nerves communicate with muscle cells. That junction is, obviously, the heart of *neuro-muscular* disease. It is also where I am about to give you my layman's best shot at explaining why ALS is so very different from IBM while at the same time so very connected...where I explain what the "I" and "B" in "IBM" mean...and how ALS is, if you follow the trail of clues and acronyms, the reason I wound up in Baltimore seeking my best possible outcome with inclusion body myositis.

What Lou Gehrig did not know as his Iron Horse streak came to its painful, tragic end is that the motor neurons controlling his muscles were dying. He was one of the world's most gifted athletes, but all the great hand/eye playmaking decisions in the world became useless as neurons failed to get instinctive messages through to his once powerful muscles. That is ALS. When an IBM patient's muscles fail, it's not because of anything wrong with the motor neurons, but because the neurons are trying to communicate with muscle cells that are themselves dying. They are different diseases with bad outcomes observable on either side of the same junction: where nerve tells muscle what to do and muscle responds.

Knowledge about IBM (and countless other medical science issues) fast-forwarded when the electron microscope came on the scene. This is what put the "inclusion body" in the "myositis." You now have enough background to follow along when I tell you that the IBM "body" is not a reference to the human body. Inclusion bodies are aggregates of abnormal proteins inside human cells. They are seen only under the most powerful microscopes or with special stains. With IBM, they are accumulations of rogue proteins within muscle cells. The bad news is that I am not qualified to explain how these inclusion bodies wound up in the muscle cells controlling my thighs and fingers The further bad news is that people who *are* qualified, like Tom Lloyd, are still working on it. The good news is that they are learning a lot.

It was Dr. Lloyd's longtime interest in amyotrophic lateral sclerosis that led him to pursue his residency at Johns Hopkins, where he could receive the very best training in neuromuscular diseases while participating in one of the world's top ALS research programs. He was happily adding to the body of knowledge about hereditary aspects of ALS and still only 35 years old when he began that one-year fellowship at JHU's brand-new Myositis Center.

Good accidents do happen. The Myositis Center was focusing on dermatomyositis and polymyositis, the treatable and collectively more prevalent types. Inclusion body myositis cases nonetheless made their way to the clinic door, referred by practitioners who had rarely encountered a case. Word of mouth and national media attention for the Myositis Center increased the stream of patients. As a result, ALS researcher Tom Lloyd saw many myositis patients, especially IBM patients, and "read" a lot of biopsies—meaning he wrote muscle biopsy pathology reports based on his interpretation of viewing slides—which at Johns Hopkins are all conducted by neuromuscular experts. In this steady flow of myositis patients Tom Lloyd the physician saw an unmet need. Tom Lloyd the scientist meanwhile reviewed the literature and realized that the underlying cause of IBM was completely unknown. And there is your good accident of time and place. Tom Lloyd became quite interested in inclusion body myositis.

Around the same time, and making Dr. Lloyd even more interested in IBM, some overlap between ALS and IBM was becoming apparent at that junction of neuron and muscle cell. For one exciting example, a certain gene in cases of hereditary IBM (more rare than my sporadic sIBM) displayed mutations identical to those found in rare inherited cases of ALS. One member of a family would develop ALS, and another would develop IBM. Mutations in this gene called Valosin Containing Protein (VCP) are known to cause a number of degenerative diseases (including front temporal dementia!). In this way a particular gene became a knowable reference point for research. An infinite number of dots remain for science to connect, which is the way research goes, and I am not qualified to explain the handful of dots already connected. But I think you can almost see my mind boggling at real progress that is being made, whether or not any practical application arrives during my lifetime. I'm pleased and proud that I managed to web-surf my own statistics right into the middle of it. The JHU Myositis Center sits a couple miles off the main Johns Hopkins University campus, amid a typical health-care layout of brick clinic buildings interspersed with parking garages and pedestrian overpasses. One building, in case you forget you are in Baltimore and the harbor is not far away, is named the Francis Scott Key Pavilion. No matter what direction you approach the Myositis Center from, it does not look like a mountaintop cave. You don't envision robed gurus greeting you. No matter. I was excited to walk in the door.

It was September 1, 2017. Tom Lloyd and I met for the first time, and he interviewed me about my history with sIBM. "Stunned" is an overstatement, but he and the Johns Hopkins crew were indeed impressed to discover that an 80-year-old guy several years after his IBM diagnosis was flying around the country, working 60 hours a week, sitting on corporate boards, leading the life I've described. Ironically, that's why, for the moment, they could not do a whole lot for me. Staff performed all the high-tech measures of muscle intensity, setting benchmarks for my next visit six months later. When IBM begins tightening its vice, Johns Hopkins personnel will help me cope. Until then, "forewarned is forearmed" pretty much covered *we'll handle my problem* in September 2017.

I was at the foremost myositis facility and in the hands of the foremost myositis gurus. I was glad to be there and should have felt very, very good when I walked out the door. Instead, the flight home ranked, though only briefly, among the biggest downers of my entire experience with inclusion body myositis. That was entirely my fault.

I had walked into the Myositis Center upright, unassisted, without so much as a cane for reassurance. I walked back out the same way. While inside the clinic I saw, for the first time, IBM patients who could *not* walk in, could not walk out, and in fact could not stand up from their wheelchairs. If I stared at them, or even gave a long sideways glance, let me apologize right now. It probably happened that way. But if you were there that day you need to know I was not staring at you. I didn't even see you. I was vain enough, as a guy who spent most of a century imagining he would live forever, to get a psychological kick in the ass by seeing myself instead of seeing you when I looked at that wheelchair. No doctor sitting across a table giving me bad news with mere words could even approach that moment of reckoning. I would in fact be in that wheelchair someday, almost without a doubt. I had climbed the right mountain, but still, just as in the cartoons, there was no magic fix.

I'm not proud of the self-pity I felt. But there you are. I flew back to Michigan in a funk.

The glumness didn't last long. Things were looking decent in a matter of hours. A day later, my outlook improved still more. Before the weekend was over I discovered what I expect to be my bearings for the remainder of this most interesting voyage.

7

ONE-EYED KINGS

*Sometimes things go spectacularly well.
Sometimes things go spectacularly bad. Most
often things go somewhere in between.*

❦

SPOILER ALERT: RELIGION WILL BE MENTIONED HERE.
The mention will be favorable.

Warning to fellow Christians: Ours is not
the only religion that will be favorably mentioned.

Good news for atheists: You don't need any
religion at all to sail on this boat. But you will
need an anchor that is bigger than yourself.

There. Now I can tell you, without risking
loss of readers, that I was raised on Catholic
Point, a sliver of a neighborhood lying between
two rivers and dominated by Holy Cross Roman

Catholic Church. That upbringing has served me well, even if my mother's mother did look me in the eye one day and say she would not waste any more time praying for me. She was 102 years old and I had taken her to lunch. Mary Brennan asked whether her busy grandson was still attending church, and the best answer I could offer was: "As often as I can get there." That was not good enough for my grandmother. She nevertheless remained eager and ready for lunch or dinner with her wayward grandson.

In fact, family and work have always ranked head and shoulders and torso above all other interests in my life. Grandma Brennan happened to catch me at a very busy time. Don't laugh. Yes, I've always been busy. But I've always tried to make weekends a time for family activities. The Highlandview Farms experiment was largely a place for family gatherings. Our place in Florida and our former place in Maine always have been family destinations, not just Jim and Joan destinations. It would not be true to say I never allowed anything but work to intrude on weekdays and never let work intrude on weekends. It would, however, be closer to truth than to fiction.

Despite my love of skiing, Maine and Florida were easy choices over, say, Utah and Colorado. That's because water has always been a powerful magnet for this family. The magnetism didn't begin with vacation or recreation. It began with occupation.

Two uncles were chief engineers on Great Lakes freighters. Another uncle was a captain. A cousin was a fleet chief. The mariner branches of the family tree trace to a time when a would-be sailor finding a berth came down almost entirely to "Who do you know?" Networking was still handy when, while I was still in high school, my Uncle Bert got me a summer job as a coalpasser on the SS Mataafa, which he served as chief engineer officer. Each voyage that season began at a dock on Detroit's east side, where we loaded new Big Three sedans and station wagons into two holds, more onto the deck, and a few more onto a flying bridge. The Mataafa then sailed down the Detroit River, across Lake Erie to Buffalo, where it unloaded. I was 16 years old, a fact that today would put my employers on the wrong side of numerous labor laws.

Everyone on and around lakes carriers refers to these vessels as boats, not ships, though many are larger than most ocean freighters. The Mataafa, launched in 1899, was 430 feet long. Average length for a Great Lakes carrier is 600 to 700 feet. A handful built since I came ashore reach 1,000 feet. Life sailing the inland sea was a learning experience not available on any campus. One day that first season I mouthed off to a fireman and he punched me in the nose. Hard. Uncle Bert took me aside and forcefully suggested that for the rest of the summer he was not to hear one word from, or about, the kid in the engine room. In September when I returned to shore and began 10th grade, two superlatives about my summer job were undeniable. First, I had learned words no nun would ever want to hear. Second, I was, compared to my peers, as rich as it gets. Three months "working on the boats" produced income approaching what my father made in a year.

It should be no surprise that I grew up on Water Street in a town named Marine City. Such richly symbolic signage surrounded me from birth, so I paid no notice. Marine City and Algonac, two small communities on the American side of the St. Clair River, were home to more Great Lakes sailors than any other addresses from Toronto to Chicago. Water Street ran along the river. The big boats passed day and night, upbound to Lake Huron and points beyond, downbound to Lake Erie—or maybe just far enough to unload iron ore at the Ford Motor

Co. Rouge Plant on Detroit's southern edge.

My parents graduated in the same class from Marine City Holy Cross High School. Vergil and Marie McTevia didn't stray far, raising my three brothers and me in a house three doors from the high school, four doors from the convent, five doors from the grade school, six doors from the church, seven doors from the rectory. My brothers and I had no excuse for being late to school or to mass, even in a blizzard.

Despite the motivational skills of stern-faced nuns, I was at best an average student all the way from first grade until the day in 1954 when Holy Cross High handed me a diploma. Perhaps I was most attentive to the religious side of my education during the puberty ritual of sneaking up to the church balcony to hear the sisters give girl students their "sex lecture." As for the secular world, I didn't think a whole lot about my future. When I collected my diploma I was a veteran of the Great Lakes fleet and at the same time I was just a 17-year-old kid. I probably intended to keep sailing and, as a result, keep being rich.

Midnight mass on Christmas Eve was a huge tradition. The rest of the year I was as devotional as the average kid in the parish, which is to say my religion was more habitual than spiritual. I was no Holy Joe, as the seriously religious were often called in that time and place. Not for a moment did it occur to me to become a priest, a thought entertained at least briefly by many boys in those days, pursued at seminary by some, and completed with ordination by a select few. Legal adulthood arrived at age 21, but by age 19 I had spent four summers among hard drinkers and carousers who swore like sailors because they *were* sailors. Still, when I came ashore for good and got married I was not yet old enough to vote.

Sailor and indifferent worshiper or not, I qualified as a believer, a young man from a family of believers, a person shaped by the rituals and moral ideals of a Catholic Point upbringing. It was a good bet that I would not hold up a liquor store, would spend my life doing my best to support my family, and would—insufficient as my Grandmother Mary Brennan might find my commitment—make it to mass as often as I could...and maybe confession, too.

Like most people, I was launched into adult life with the values of my upbringing and man-aged to hold onto most. Marriage and acquir-ing my own family—three sons, one daughter, and eight grandchildren—gradually made me a more serious person. So did tragedies and close calls that happened to friends and loved ones. At the office I routinely encountered profound personal despair among clients. Regardless what route we choose, each of us walks an ever more serious journey through life. Do we get older and wiser? We like to think so. Older, for sure. Did I get more religious as the years and the experiences piled on? Yeah. Did I at last become a Holy Joe? No. Not close. But if I could take Grandma Brennan to lunch tomorrow, she would probably relent and resume praying for my soul.

That's true even though—after telling her I had become more spiritual and more attendant to the rituals of my religion—I would also tell her that much of any progress I've made toward being a less flawed human being has come from the secular world and from people who practice a different religion, or none at all. More on that later. But this is where I want to explain the role my Catholic Point upbringing played in chasing away, almost overnight, the nagging depression that tried to gain traction as I left the Johns Hopkins Myositis Center on September 1, 2017.

Early that year is when I fell while walking Murphy. Then came the disastrous parking lot tumble that had my kids asking why I kept my elbows and knees hidden in beautiful late-spring weather. On June 23, I resumed acupuncture treatment and, as you know, stopped falling. Six days before that I served for the first time as lector during Saturday mass at Holy Cross Church on Catholic Point, seven miles south of our current home on the river. Three months later I flew off to Baltimore and Johns Hopkins with body *and* spirit in good shape. Acupuncture, I am convinced, accounted for the body component of my upbeat attitude. The spirit part—the spiritual part—had been building for decades. Serving as lector for the first time makes a good mile marker.

A lector is a congregation member who reads scripture during a religious service. In the Roman Catholic Church, a cycle of scripture readings is chosen several years in advance. Parishioners who volunteer as lectors are prepped in projecting their voices, so worshipers can hear, and in understanding the scripture they recite, so as to deliver it convincingly. Lectoring is a serious commitment, not sought by many. I'm told my voice carries well in the Holy Cross sanctuary, that my understanding of the day's scripture is apparent, and that my earnest delivery sustains attention. With reviews like that, even if only a handful show up for Saturday mass it feels like an ecclesiastical Yankee Stadium to me.

How does a teenaged sailor visiting bawdy bars in Indiana steel mill ports become an octogenarian who gives public scripture readings? Well, six additional decades of life's lessons... realizing you won't live another eight decades... wondering where inclusion body myositis will take you, and when—the long list of obvious answers can be summed up, I think, in two large, useful lessons. First, you *will* run into a problem you can't solve. Second, no matter what a hotshot you might be in your day job, outcomes are never all about you.

Many regard me as a master problem-solver. Fine. I accept. Proud to hear it. But the longer I've walked that path, and the better I've gotten at my profession, the more I've realized that first big lesson: Sooner or later we all— even professional problem-solvers—run into a problem we can't solve, or sidestep, or reshape, or even dent. Inclusion body myositis qualifies. The second big lesson has been revealing itself incrementally all my life—as it does, I think, for almost everyone. We find it in different ways, in different places, in our own good time. But it is a universal truth.

For me, it went this way. My clients confront fundamentally identical situations but come out the other side with wildly different results. Sometimes things go spectacularly well. Sometimes things go spectacularly bad. Most often things go somewhere in between. I do the best I can for all clients, and there you have my "problem-solver" reputation. But let's not forget that nine clients killed themselves. Just halfway through my career it was already becoming clearer and clearer to me that some unseen power, some force, has a bigger hand in running the show than Jim McTevia. It's not something I understand—which is the whole point, no? All the great religions (and many great thinkers who adhere to no particular religion) come to the same conclusion, that no matter who we are, some larger force shapes the script of our lives. My church solves that mystery for me, and I embrace its teachings. But humanity sails on a very large boat, and great truths have a way of crossing boundaries.

My personal bottom line: Old Jim McTevia is a believer in a way young Jim McTevia was not. On many days, for example, I take great comfort, and learn a lot, listening for 15 or 20 minutes to homilies written and delivered by a priest I've never met. You could say it's my Catholic Point childhood reaching maturity 70 years later—on iTunes, no less—via a church in San Luis Obispo, California. I learned about Father Matt Pennington's homilies from a friend who said Pennington has an energetic and enjoyable way of illuminating scripture with experience and common sense. Maybe I would enjoy listening? Yes, on all counts. I've developed several favorite Pennington homilies that I re-run from time to time, plus each week's new installment. The one that has meant the most to me arrived in an almost magical bit of good timing.

I flew back from Baltimore brooding because that was as good as it was going to get. I had been to the top of the myositis mountain but my IBM was only going to be managed, not cured, perhaps not even slowed down. My Johns Hopkins visit was a reality check. This airborne brooding might have become nasty, but the next day a family weekend began at our house on the river. Kids and grandkids showed up. We all had a good time. It was great medicine. When the last guest left on Sunday, I sat down and surfed the Internet. I was already feeling good. And then pure gold popped onto my laptop.

A new homily had just been uploaded from the Nativity of Our Lady Catholic Community, Father Pennington's parish. It's available free in the iTunes catalogue, dated September 4,

2017. It's entitled: GOD IS GOOD

Pennington speaks in his little sermon of watching how network news covered Hurricane Harvey's destruction in Houston, and how aggravating it is when a TV reporter sticks a microphone in someone's face on the worst day of their life and asks: "How do you feel?" But like most of us in times of great disaster, Father Pennington watches, transfixed. And in the hurricane's wake he saw people "all in the same situation but their response to it is really quite different. Some people have been flattened by what's going on, have no hope, have no faith, they're just completely bereft...just sitting there stunned, waiting for someone to tell them what to do and where to go. Other people who are in the same situation seem to have tremendous courage, resiliency, optimism, and hope and faith—people in the same situation responding so very differently."

You can see how that observation resonated with this alleged master problem-solver.

Then Father Pennington reached 2,500 miles to my easy chair on the St. Clair River, cutting straight to the heart of how I have decided to deal with my decaying muscles and my unsolvable problem. Here was a genuine Holy Joe, empowered to administer every rite of the church but also infectiously enthusiastic about greeting every sunrise. The homily, in fact, sealed my resolve to write a book about my IBM experience—and, for good measure, inspired the book's title.

Father Pennington laid out a checklist of things I've counseled to clients for decades. One Houston family's house was destroyed by the hurricane's flood. They had just moved in after losing their previous home in a fire. The husband nonetheless is eager to thank rescue and cleanup volunteers for their great work. The wife points at the rubble that once was their household treasure, looks into the camera and says: "This is just *stuff*. We're OK, and that's what matters. We'll find a new home and build new memories...because God is good."

It's ironic that I always tell despairing clients every word of that quote except the last three: "God is good." I'm not a preacher and not a Holy Joe, just a turnaround management guy who has helped hundreds of people cope with financial disaster. Those who understand that being alive is a great gift, that Land Rovers and sprawling homes in the country are "just *stuff*," are the ones who not only survive catastrophe but more often than not thrive in its wake. I have absolutely no problem giving God a lot of credit for good outcomes, although I don't advise "God is good" as part of my consulting. My role is to point the way toward the best possible outcomes from a vantage point down here on the ground. As a believer, I have no difficulty understanding that a larger force has a powerful hand in the endeavor.

As Father Pennington preaches about people facing identical circumstances but emerging with wildly different outcomes, he says of the Houston woman who lost her home for the second time (my italics): "Isn't that extraordinary... to say in that moment that 'God is good.' I think *the response of that Texas woman is the answer to the mystery of life.*"

Grandma Brennan, there you are. Your grandson who wasn't making it to church often enough has been busy, in a secular way all these years, teaching the mystery of life! Well, not exactly. But if financial solutions are often breathtakingly simple ("Take in more money, or spend less money, or do both"), then an even simpler truth I've always tried to help clients understand ("It's only stuff") is the secret of life. Actually the good father was focusing on the "God is good" clause. That's OK. I'm on board with that, too.

Now for the part that inspired the three

words in big type on this book's cover.

Pennington talks about his dermatologist finding a cancerous growth beneath his right eye, removing it, and then monitoring to see if it has spread outward. The doctor didn't say Pennington might lose his eye, not exactly, but pretty soon the priest "began to envision that maybe I am going to lose my eye, and pretty soon I became convinced." He told this to a parishioner named Jackie, who fired back: "Well, if you lose your eye at least you have another one."

Father Pennington urges his congregation: "Let me tell you something Jackie understands: In the land of the blind, the one-eyed man is king...She's right. I have another eye. Even if I were to be made blind through this process, how grateful I am to have been able to see the wonders and the vistas that God has put before me...And in that moment, through a certain amount of uncertainty, I knew God was good."

At the end of the homily, Father Pennington challenges his California flock: "So which one will you be when the floods come, or the earthquake? How will you respond when it is time for you to pick up *your* cross? Because right this minute you have everything you need to survive, to thrive to find peace and fulfillment. And remember: *In the land of the blind, the one-eyed man will be the king.*"

If I had a monster pipe organ in our house on the river, it might as well have been cued for soaring accompaniment right there. Grandma Brennan might have said: "Bingo!" It's not exactly true that a priest on iTunes decided how I plan to stare down whatever future setbacks I might face along every step—or misstep—of the way. The homily echoes what I've learned and counseled for decades in the secular world. But never, ever underestimate the power of a good homily to summon intense clarity and help sort things out.

Most of us at some time will be diminished by a disease, or a disability, or the sudden obsolescence of a career we had been counting on, or by being wronged, or by being in the wrong place at the wrong time. We need to keep in mind, for starters, that world population now approaches 8 billion human beings, many millions of them starving, or living under brutal totalitarian regimes, or amid the carnage of military conflict, or pennies-a-day poverty—or all of the above. All these millions would, in a flash, trade places with the woman in Houston who said her family would be "OK." She understood.

The clarity of a quarter-hour spent listening to Matt Pennington's homily has helped me focus on how at my age I have already experienced so much good in this world...that perhaps acupuncture granted me an extra year or two of full mobility...that even after several years living with IBM, most people in my world don't realize I have it...that I am doing my work as always, and plan to continue doing so if I wind up in a wheelchair. It's only a plan, mind you, not a guarantee. But it's a *solid* plan. I am one determined old sailor. That's not bragging. It's advice—because it looks like the best path forward not just for me, but for anyone. We all, as long as circumstances allow us to put one foot in front of the other—literally OR figuratively—will be OK. Amid our difficulties and deficits, we will be One-Eyed Kings.

Thank you, Father Pennington, for the clarity.

As 2017 drew to a close I served as lector at Christmas midnight mass. It was a deeply fulfilling moment. Once again I got good reviews. All the reviews came from people I know, but good ink is good ink.

When the holiday pause ended, I returned full-time to life as a business consultant. In the secular world, clients and colleagues might or might not be religious, something I usually don't know—as they usually don't know about me. All my life I've learned, without benefit of religious guidance, a lot about humanity's failings and its potential.

Humility, for example and as far as I know, is a virtue encouraged by all the great religions and by any philosophy worth heeding. I certainly learned some humility in the Mataafa engine room when that fireman punched me in the nose. And the simple declaration, "I am a person too," voiced from a parking attendant's booth in Miami, made this hotshot problem-solver a little less arrogant for the rest of his life, long before he volunteered to read scripture at mass.

It's a wondrous world. I'm happy to be in it. I'm a little embarrassed that sometimes the words "inclusion body myositis" let me forget how wondrous it is. I'll be working on that, as I might tell Grandma Brennan, "as often as I can."

8

'I'D RATHER NOT HAVE INCLUSION BODY MYOSITIS'

I've bought into to the idea that I am not going to live forever, but as long as I'm breathing I would prefer to live full-bore.

AFTER SIX MONTHS I RETURNED to the Johns Hopkins Myositis Center for a second session of flexing fingers, lifting legs, and otherwise testing muscle strength. Traveling to be examined at a facility devoted to a rare disease is a deeply personal thing. It simultaneously reminds you of having been singled out by fate but it also makes you feel pampered, or at least not ignored. Meanwhile, the finger flexing and leg lifting become an anonymous, communal contribution to science. Each IBM pilgrim's metrics flow into a data trove, a longitudinal study being assembled by Johns Hopkins researchers. Ultimately the data gathered will be an important part of progress in treating IBM.

The night before this trip's first appointment I strolled down the street to a restaurant near my hotel. The one-block expedition amounted to a much less scientific measure of my physical status on February 28, 2018. As a practical assessment, however, it offered all the clarity of a fine camera lens.

I walked without a cane, as I still do at this writing. A careful observer might have said that at moments my gait resembled an actor's idea of how an 81-year-old walks. In truth, if I did not have IBM most observers would have guessed me to be a decade or two younger, which is how most people describe my overall appearance. Skilled physicians and therapists, on the other hand, amaze me with their ability to spot and classify disabilities among the patients who knock on their door. Tom Lloyd utilizes the full range of diagnostic protocols before officially declaring a new patient has IBM. More than 90 percent of the time, however, he knows what the verdict will be after a minute or less spent personally testing finger and hand strength and movement.

Neither expertise nor guesswork was necessary to see that I couldn't step up onto the curb outside the restaurant in Baltimore's Inner Harbor. Almost all curbs had become a challenge. This one appeared to be an inch higher than average, putting it in Mt. Everest territory—just as the next morning I would impress a therapist by standing up from a seated position, but would flunk the same test a moment later when he lowered the seat one inch. I had learned to negotiate curbs either by finding a sign pole to grasp for leverage and security, or by walking along the gutter until I found a wheelchair ramp. On this night I sidestepped and grabbed a post.

Gripping a sign pole deploys a slightly different set of muscles and tendons than gripping a knife and fork to cut a piece of meat, a skill I lost many months before this dinner. I ordered a nice cut of beef and asked the server to have it sliced for me in the kitchen. Restaurant workers these days are seldom taken aback by such a request, which suggests it is not as unusual as I imagined when my cutlery skills began to vanish. I always ask nonetheless for the slicing to be done out of sight of other restaurant patrons. At family gatherings one of our brood does the task for me right at the table. The family understands Gramps has a problem, though only lately have they begun to realize how much of a problem.

That's the familiar psychology. Embarrassment. Fear of not being able to keep up. The vague but powerful dread of deviating from normal. All three negative emotions keep trying to inflict pain on those debilitated by disease. Such thoughts can't be fought off 24/7. Not so far as I've noticed. Maybe by a saint, but not by an old ordinary seaman.

Six months after finding my north star in a Matt Pennington homily, I was still complaining to myself about my situation. I still do, often enough, despite my best efforts. I confess without hesitation to this sin. It's a well-established fact that I would rather not have inclusion body myositis. I've bought into the idea that I am not going to live forever, but as long as I'm breathing I would prefer to live full-bore. You may take that as whining disguised as wit, or simply as straightforward reporting on how the human psyche functions...saints and liars excepted. The Inner Harbor dinner, however, was fine. No complaints. The curb had not grown another inch when I returned to the hotel. IBM is not the worst disease in the world, and I didn't even have its most advanced symptoms. When I put my head on the pillow that night I realized, as I do most of the time, that I *am* a one-eyed king.

The next day a physical therapist and an occupational therapist recorded more measurements than the most meticulous tailor. The following morning, Dr. Lloyd performed a few more tests during our consultation. His verdict? A few muscle functions were actually a bit stronger than six months earlier—no doubt because my exercise regimen had helped healthy muscles strengthen to perform tasks they were never intended to do. Early in the brief history of IBM it was believed that exercise was a bad idea. Live and learn. Moderation in all things. IBM patients fare best if they exercise, with doctors and therapists coaching which muscles to work out, and how much.

Sitting in an exam room in my skivvies, looking at my wasted quadriceps muscles and the shrunken mass in my forearms, it was good to know that other muscles were trying to compensate. Nice—but no solution, merely an organized retreat from normal strength and mobility. On this day I won a skirmish, but I would not be opening pickle jars again, or approaching stairs with anything but trepidation. Stepping downstairs sideways in the morning while grasping a rail had already become standard procedure. At the end of the day, I usually headed upstairs straight ahead—but adding security and saving time by navigating on hands and knees.

I reported that kind of personal detail to Dr. Lloyd and insisted I was determined to regard IBM as a mere "irritant." I told him I still had not encountered a client who refused to pay for expertise because I wore buttonless garments. Tom Lloyd sees patients almost every week whose disabilities are far more advanced than mine, so he probably was not as impressed by my little speech as I was.

Johns Hopkins had launched several interesting clinical trials, Lloyd said, and would be launching more. Would I be interested? I repeated the methotrexate saga, my lone experience with unproven drug therapies and possible side effects. Methotrexate made me adamant that despite the potential upside of any drug trial, the downside was enough for me to say, always and unequivocally: "No thanks." No medication, for IBM or any other malady, would be crossing my lips or injected into my butt unless it was in common and effective use without causing near-death experiences. This attitude might be bullheaded. It is not, however, irrational. Some say I am a bullheaded but very rational kind of guy.

Dr. Lloyd and I talked, of course, about my experience with acupuncture. I voiced the full-throated endorsement you now know by heart. Science can't explain why many IBM patients find acupuncture helpful. Science, so far, does not come down forcefully on either side of "acupuncture is a definite physical aid for IBM patients" vs. "acupuncture is probably a placebo." The physician/scientist Tom Lloyd does not scoff at acupuncture. Many patients find it helpful. Some, like me, regard it as vital. Dr. Lloyd entertains several possible theories, one of which involves acupuncture playing a role in strengthening muscles not affected by IBM. What matters to me is that here is a guy who spends most of his time immersed in science, meaning he is like me a "show me" skeptic in his area of expertise—but he does not turn his back on anecdotal evidence that has not been disproven and is neither harmful nor quixotic.

As Dr. Lloyd measured my ability, while sitting, to lift a leg against resistance, I found myself staring—as I sometimes do—at the hollowed spaces, formerly muscle, on either side of my upper legs. Dr. Lloyd approved of my lifting effort, and pointed at a ridge of muscle between the hollows and running to my kneecap.

It's a classic IBM pattern, Dr. Lloyd said. Three muscles waste away, while one quadriceps remains whole and provides support and motion, however weakly and unreliably and for however long. What a very, very incredible stream of events among neurons and muscle cells and body chemistry and sometimes genes must be required to produce such an odd result—and then do it again and again among that small number of us with IBM. In its unkind way, such predictable mayhem is as amazing as more welcome scenes on the vast canvass painted by God and nature.

And there comes our old friend human nature stepping boldly, as usual, into the picture as I bemoan my six withered quadriceps muscles. Don't I realize the much more terrible nature of other diseases that can strike any of us at any time? Of course. I had friends and loved ones who were taken by worse diseases than IBM. How about fatal accidents (what an interesting word "accident" is, as if a happenstance is mere happenstance, regardless of degree)? Of course. I have seen the least expectable sort of accident rob good friends of their child. How about others with inclusion body myositis who this afternoon cannot walk across a room, let alone out the door of the Johns Hopkins Myositis Center, as I did when Dr. Lloyd finished his consultation? Of course. Several times a day I concede all the things that could be worse for me. And *still* I'd rather not have IBM.

Nobody ever said the great truth about One-Eyed Kings doesn't require tending and nourishing as a constant reminder. With a disease like IBM, it should be easy—well, relatively easy—to keep Matt Pennington's proverbial message in mind. It takes only slight effort to look around and see someone worse off. The slow and inescapable nature of IBM's progressive curse, however, does make it a chore to prevent your disease from becoming the focal point of your day. You can, after all, choose what you have for breakfast and dinner, but the same old IBM is going to be there every morning and every night. So you need to work at it constantly. You need to focus elsewhere. Sometimes, even at 81, it's good to be a workaholic.

As I wrapped up my biannual visit to Baltimore, the first of a series of 2018 nor'easters was slamming into the mid-Atlantic states. Young and healthy people were being whipped in the wind, like the traffic signs they walked past. As I left, Dr. Lloyd was worrying about IBM patients making their way from car to clinic. Baltimore commuter trains were canceled all day.

Hundreds of flights were canceled out of New York. But my flight to Florida took me south safely and on schedule. It had been a good trip, what with the thumbs-up on my muscle benchmarks and all. I settled in for the night thinking about an upcoming business week that included, among other things, a trip to Canada for a corporate board meeting.

The next morning I tumbled down the stairs of our home in Jupiter.

The stairs are carpeted. I wasn't hurt. In the following week I fulfilled all items on my agenda. All went normally in the outside world. But in the Saturday morning privacy at the bottom of our staircase, it was an emotional moment. All those thoughts and fears about where IBM might be taking you, and when, sail across your mind—twice—quicker than you can check for broken bones. That's probably because such thoughts and fears about the future are a bigger psychic priority, believe it or not, than the condition of your collarbone at the moment.

Embarrassment? Hey, not quite 24 hours earlier I was in Baltimore explaining to one of the world's foremost myositis experts how acupuncture was keeping me on my feet. Now, gathering myself and standing up, it felt as if my Johns Hopkins bragging points were playing on all the cable news channels, along with video of me tumbling down the stairs.

This, my friends, is why "living in the moment" is not something to be taken literally. Living in today, on the other hand, might be the very heart of any first-class coping mechanism. One day is a manageable thing. One moment, not so much. So I pushed myself past a very bad moment and on into my day, and then into my week.

The facts of IBM's progression were not to be denied. But neither was the fact that it had been almost four months since my previous fall, one of two in rapid succession that I attributed to unusual stress and to having strayed away from acupuncture. Had I gotten the idea that I would never fall again? Not at all. Was I hoping the next fall would have happened at a somewhat less humiliating time? Yes; but we know life doesn't cooperate that way. Did falling again after four months add up to some kind of arithmetical indication I would fall again in two months, or two weeks, or two days? Absolutely not. Had I become just a millisecond careless in my regimen for descending stairs, perhaps goaded by my successful Baltimore trip? I doubt it, but who knows. So what does one do? Well, you resume life, one day at a time.

And on this particular day I had the benefit of it being quite likely that the worst part of my day was already over.

By dinnertime IBM remained a mere irritant. I would have insisted on that if you asked. IBM was a damned large irritant. But just an irritant.

A few days later, the pilot helped me up into the Navajo and I flew to that Ontario board meeting. Absolutely nothing that transpired that busy week went any differently than if I had bounded down the stairs Saturday morning like a kid looking forward to his cartoon shows.

9

A PSYCHIATRIST, TWO PRIESTS, AND JOE WALSH

*We cope in our own ways, borrowing good
ideas from others. Nothing wrong with that.
I obviously hope you are finding a few things
worth borrowing from these pages.*

❧

IN THE LATE 1970S A PSYCHIATRIST WROTE a book-length prescription for living happily and productively. A major publisher rejected it, saying one section of the manuscript was "too Christ-y." The psychiatrist eventually found a publisher, but the book gained no traction in the marketplace. The author went on the lecture circuit, sold books at the back of the room, solicited reviews, beat every drum he could find to support his book and its message. This was two decades before the Internet allowed authors to connect instantaneously with everyone on the planet. The psychiatrist, M. Scott Peck, found traction for his book nonetheless. *The Road Less Traveled* has now sold more than 10 million copies.

I've never thought of *The Road Less Traveled* as a religious book. I've mostly thought of it as a compelling, useful book emphasizing a simple, vital, fundamental truth that is too often ignored—life is difficult. I give a copy to clients who face serious adversity, which is to say most of my clients. Human beings caught in a bad place tend to dwell on the wildly mistaken, smothering idea that they have been singled out for ill fortune. My clients—and me, and probably you—are no exception. Breaking out of that cycle, understanding that life is difficult and we are not the only one facing adversity, is like breaking through a Great Lakes ice jam.

Joan and I read *The Road Less Traveled* soon after it became a best-seller. We attended one of Peck's seminars, became active in his Foundation for Community Encouragement, and became close enough friends to call him Scotty. Best-selling authors are besieged by requests to lend support to other authors' books, often responding with a one-paragraph dust-jacket blurb. Peck, who died in 2005, wrote only one foreword for another author. That was for my own *Bankrupt: A Society Living in the Future*, published in 1992. It was a great honor to discover that a psychiatrist whose books flew off the shelves like a startled flock of sparrows was informing the world: "I write this foreword because here is a book about sanity."

Bankrupt's core message—Americans are burying themselves in a dark hole by refusing to stop plunging into unrealistic debt—was so painfully true, and remains so painfully true, that no one wants to hear it. I can assure you that writing a book about a problem so toxic no one will read about is not a path to the bestseller list, M. Scott Peck's endorsement notwithstanding.

When *Bankrupt* was published, I flew down to Washington and hand-delivered copies to the offices of all 435 members of the U.S. House of Representatives, to all 100 senators, and to Vice-President Al Gore—so he would have some reading material while waiting to cast a tie-breaking vote in the Senate. Condensing a lifetime spent closely observing the peril of runaway debt into a book, then offering that warning to the nation's elected officials, was no doubt the most impractical thing I've ever done. My company's PR consultant and good friend, the late Fred Marx, accompanied me on my D.C. rounds. Fred, a master of gracious understatement, described *Bankrupt*'s wakeup call as "politely ignored." Not only did members of Congress keep right on living ever larger into the future, a Florida congressman and Al Gore were the only two of the 536 Washington recipients who mailed me so much as a "thanks for the book." Not one national news organization—not even C-Span—took note of my bookmobile lobbying on behalf of sanity.

Not one to be discouraged regarding an issue that I believe could bring a great nation to its knees, and lower, I doubled down and produced another book, *The Culture of Debt: How a Once-Proud Society Mortgaged Its Future*. This time, I was convinced, common sense and the peril facing our grandchildren would provide traction for a vital message. No such luck. Publishing is an interesting and challenging business.

Now, a quarter century after Mr. McTevia went to Washington, a few politicians and commentators can be heard every day insisting that our refusal to live within our means is stealing our grandchildren's future. Meanwhile they do nothing about it and in fact double down in their extravagance. This is, Scott Peck said and I continue to believe, pathological behavior, fiscal madness. But I've spoken my piece on the subject. I had no intention of ever writing another book. Then I had occasion to hear the words "inclusion body myositis" spoken with no one else in the room to answer the call. So here's another book.

If *Bankrupt* was a book about sanity, and if *The Road Less Traveled* was at heart a book about realizing that life is difficult, what is *One-Eyed Kings*? Both. This is not a book about IBM in any expert medical sense (except shortly when Dr. Tom Lloyd's afterword offers an overview of myositis science and treatment). So let's call *One-Eyed Kings* a little book of true tales and helpful hints about staying sane along the difficult path we call life. Inclusion body myositis is the most difficult problem I've faced. I've coped by starting with the fact that life is difficult, that I have not been singled out for ill fortune, and that I've got so many good things going for me that I am a king—though one-eyed, so to speak.

You've had your own big problem, medical or otherwise. We both might yet face worse. Or not. We cope in our own ways, borrowing good ideas from others. Nothing wrong with that. I obviously hope you are finding a few things worth borrowing from these pages.

It's important to me that non-Christian or non-religious friends and readers not think *One-Eyed Kings* is too religious just because I borrow from Father Matt Pennington and from my Catholic Point upbringing. I sure don't see it that way—any more than the lesson I borrowed from a Miami parking lot attendant was too... what...*mundane*? Most lessons I've learned lately were taught by inclusion body myositis. Filtered, of course, through a Catholic Point childhood but also the engine rooms of Great Lakes freighters, a brief life as a repo man, a long career as a finance problem-solver, and life experiences as a father and grandfather. These days I attend church as a believer, and once a week I find Matt Pennington's homilies more relaxing than the wasteland that fills 95 percent of TV airtime. Trust me when I insist that a mother lode of earthly lessons can be mined from religious sources.

Not long after my first visit to Johns Hopkins, for example, I attended Sunday mass in Florida. It was the first day of a retreat, an occasion for bringing in well-regarded special speakers, which is why I drove down to Our Lady of Florida Spiritual Center. I have forgotten the name of the priest who gave the introductory homily. We have never crossed paths before or since. Within a minute or two he had me believing my little drive was a waste of time. I couldn't figure out where his sermon was headed. I am sure he will forgive me for not remembering his name, because I will never forget where his message led.

The priest stared hard at the assembly and asked: "Who do you think you are? Do you really think you are better than Jesus Christ?"

Oh boy. We are off, I thought, into some weeds of philosophical babble I would just as soon avoid. But the speaker quickly reeled me in with a most worldly message cloaked in religious parable. I had been thinking, obviously, about IBM and my plans for dealing with it. Matt Pennington had just bestowed on me the one-eyed-kings foundation for being at peace with my wasting muscles. Now, in another homily, I was about to get some world-class advice about how to cope proactively. It hit me in the solar plexus—or, considering my problem, in the quadriceps.

There were three crosses on Calvary that day, the priest said, but only one had been carried there by Jesus. Most people spend their days trying to carry three crosses. One is the shoulda-woulda cross, a burden of regrets and anger over things that happened in the past—

things we cannot do anything about. "Why didn't I go to college, or why did I marry so young, or why did I move to a job that almost instantly became obsolete?" Then there is the future cross, built of worries such as "will my health continue to deteriorate, or will my 401K go south, or will my spouse tire of me?"

His admonition, delivered only moments after I couldn't imagine where this priest was going, was so clear I almost could recite it in unison—as, I'm sure, most others in the church could. Focus on just one cross, he said. Focus on *today*'s burdens. That's enough. Or as my psychiatrist friend Scott Peck would say, life is difficult. Why triple your burden? Get your act together. Focus on things you can do something about...or at least cope with. Isn't that enough?

I sat enthralled, even though you might say: "Of course. That is so simple. Who needs a priest to figure that out?" You would be right. But remember, I have spent decades trying to get very successful and smart and talented people to understand that only three vectors can stop a torrent of red ink: Spend less. Increase income. Or both. And though it may seem obvious that carrying one cross is an easier burden than carrying three, the world is full of people driven into the ground by the weight of past events they can't do anything about and future situations that might, or might not, come to pass. Simple is good. Simple can be profound. And simple can hide in plain sight.

Few epiphanies, in fact, are really the fresh-minted lightning bolts they seem to be. Knowledge comes to us in increments, a continually improved understanding of simple, powerful ideas. The most worn clichés can shout out brand-new wisdom when you hold them just so, under just the best light, from just the proper angle. Suddenly they plug into your own circumstances so snugly they need no gasket. I couldn't tell you, for example, whether I found myself thinking of rock guitarist Joe Walsh as I sat in that Florida spiritual center, or even humming a particular song in my mind. I sure might have. It would have been a perfect fit.

Not to underestimate the enduring strength of the Alcoholics Anonymous motto, or the Kris Kristofferson song of the same name, but for me no one ever rendered three words—"one day at a time"—with more credentials than Joe Walsh...and definitely not with so much musical flair. I grant you that the Eagles were always a special group to my ears. I immersed myself in the spirit of Walsh's "One Day at a Time" before I ever heard of "inclusion body myositis"—partly because of troubles endured by people dear to me, partly because it is simply a good song. Besides, as I entered my 70s and discovered I had to keep networking new clients, I found both poignancy and good humor in Joe Walsh lines like...

All the friends I used to run with are gone,
Lord I hadn't planned on livin' this long.

Then when IBM came along, the song's kicker line...

I have to learn to live my life
one day at a time.

...suddenly sounded like a clear summons to reality emanating from, of all places, rock and roll. So it was no surprise that I began to hear Joe Walsh's "One Day at a Time" as my personal myositis anthem. If I hummed it subconsciously while the Florida priest imparted the wisdom of carrying just one cross, who could be surprised? The retreat-leading priest and the rocker both had struck power chords in my mind and soul. Why not a duet? Add Matt Pennington's insistence about who rules the land of the blind and I had a whole band playing truth back at me.

I'm not going to worry now about the day when I'll need a crutch or a wheelchair. I just know I'll find a way. Besides, that's in the future, and we don't really know what's in store. Nothing I can do today will change that. I'm physically and emotionally well enough to carry one cross, to let my pilot help me climb into the Navajo, and to fly off to my next board meeting. Thank you, clergy. Thank you, Joe Walsh. I also thank God, but that's my personal decision. You thank whatever greater power works for you. But I highly recommend taking it one day at a time.

Grab your today and get the most out of it. Give something back if you can. Then put your head on the pillow and sleep well. One day down, and hopes for many more to come. Treating sleep apnea if you have it is, like belief, up to you. The apnea treatment machine makes me gag, makes noise, makes me wake up feeling less refreshed than if I don't take it out of its case. My own granddaughter, who has expertise in the subject, tells me I am nuts for that. In this case you might say I am trading "stubborn but rational" for "stubborn and irrational." I'll just admit that and wake up rested. More often I accept expertise as a fine and even a wonderful thing. I chose the Johns Hopkins

Myositis Center and Dr. Lloyd to be my IBM gurus. They know as much or more as anyone in the world regarding the irritant in my life. I'll be returning to Baltimore every six months for the foreseeable future. I don't expect to find any magic there. Science, after all, is the very embodiment of what I said about epiphanies. Almost every "Eureka!" moment happens incrementally, a payoff moment that arrives only after a long research process. IBM is a rare disease, and relatively new. I am attuned to the fact that my medical case is not about curing me but, hopefully, helping find a cure for others who have not yet been told why they are having trouble buttoning shirts and writing a note.

If this manuscript becomes a book, and if the book generates enough cash flow that I am owed any royalties, every penny will go to IBM research. It would be nice if that were to happen.

Most of all, I hope others who—now and in the future—encounter a hint of unsteadiness, then realize they are undeniably and literally losing their grip, will read *One-Eyed Kings*. I hope it will encourage them to let someone else carry yesterday's cross and tomorrow's cross and focus instead on today's burden. I hope they will see that whatever deficits may come their way from IBM or any other adversity, they will be in the land of the blind and that the lesson about One-Eyed Kings is not a mere platitude. I hope that like me, when they hear...

*In the land of the blind
the one-eyed man is king.*

...they will see a palpable...*grippable*...motto for stepping forward, one day at a time.

AFTERWORD

By Dr. Tom Lloyd, M.D., Ph.D.

I SAW MY FIRST PATIENT with inclusion body myositis (IBM) in 2002, during my neurology clinical rotation as a medical student at Baylor College of Medicine in Houston. I was on my neurology rotation working with Dr. Stan Appel, a leading expert in amyotrophic lateral sclerosis (ALS). As nicely described in this book, IBM is sometimes misdiagnosed as ALS, both being untreatable, progressive degenerative diseases causing muscle atrophy and weakness. On this one-month rotation, I saw perhaps 20 ALS patients, but only one IBM patient. Given how mysterious this disease was (and is), I decided to do my rotation presentation on IBM. I still remember this patient and my presentation. Despite many theories, IBM's cause was unknown and there was no treatment. Some experts argued it was a degenerative disease like Alzheimer's or ALS. Others argued it was an autoimmune disease like other forms of myositis. This fundamental debate continues, and no treatment has yet been found.

I had just completed my Ph.D. thesis in molecular and cell biology in the laboratory of Dr. Hugo Bellen, a leading expert in using fruit fly genetics to understand the development of the peripheral nervous system. For my thesis, I studied development of the neuromuscular junction (NMJ), the synaptic connection between nerves and muscles. Toward the end of my training in the Medical Scientist Training Program, I decided to enter the field of neurology. I intended to use my expertise in neuromuscular genetics to study the cause of ALS, and seek treatments for this devastating neurodegenerative disease that typically causes death in three to five years. I chose to pursue my neurology residency and neuromuscular clinical fellowship at Johns Hopkins University School of Medicine, which was regarded as a top neurology residency program. Johns Hopkins also boasted one of the best ALS research programs in the country, led by Dr. Jeffrey Rothstein. He had formed the Robert Packard Center for ALS Research, which funded many of the world's top ALS researchers. This Johns Hopkins University community is where I learned how collaborative research among patients, scientists, and physicians could advance the field.

During my one-year neuromuscular fellowship in 2007, I decided to focus my clinical practice and research in IBM rather than ALS, for several reasons.

First, Dr. Andrew Mammen, a neurologist, and Dr. Lisa Christopher-Stine, a rheumatologist, had just launched the multidisciplinary Johns Hopkins Myositis Center. Heavy publicity for this endeavor led to a large influx of IBM referrals. This produced a marked increase in the number of new muscle biopsies performed and slides received for consultation. My job as the sole neuromuscular fellow was to interpret all these muscle biopsies. I read well over 300 biopsies that year, nearly doubling the usual census. In spending countless hours looking at slides of IBM patients under the microscope, I was amazed at how, on the one hand, there was rip-roaring inflammation as severe, if not more severe, than other forms of myositis; and yet on the other hand, there were degenerative features typical of neurodegenerative diseases such as "ubiquitinated protein aggregates" that form the appearance of "inclusions" within muscles cells on electron microscopy. Also, that very year, Drs. Chris Weihl and Steve Greenberg, two leading experts in IBM research, had reported that these protein aggregates contained a protein called TDP-43 that had recently been found to be the key protein that aggregated in motor neurons in ALS. Thus, the very same gene and protein that I had started focusing my laboratory research on using fruit fly models was now implicated in the cause of IBM.

The other forces that led to me to pursue IBM as my clinical research focus were more practical and personal. Having seen many ALS patients with Dr. Rothstein, I realized that I became overly emotionally invested in these patients' devastating diagnosis. In most cases, patients had previously been told that it was likely ALS but, given the disease's uniformly poor prognosis, had held out hope that the diagnosis was incorrect. Unfortunately, we almost always confirmed it was ALS, and we had little comfort to offer patients who received this abysmal diagnosis. At the end of a day of ALS clinic, I was emotionally drained, though the next day I would be motivated to work even harder in the lab. "The Hope is in the Science" is the motto of the Robert Packard Center for ALS Research, and enrolling these patients in clinical research and trials was probably the most empowering thing we could do for them. On the other hand, when seeing IBM patients with Dr. Mammen at the Myositis Center, I learned that this disease, while incurable, was manageable, and I really enjoyed my interactions with the patients I met.

From a practical perspective, there also wasn't a demand at Johns Hopkins for more neuromuscular neurologists to see patients in the ALS clinic. In contrast, there was a real need for another neurologist to see patients at the growing Myositis Center, especially since Drs. Mammen and Christopher-Stine focused on dermatomyositis and immune-mediated necrotizing myopathy, two other forms of myositis. Also, there seemed to me to be very little research being done in IBM. What sealed the deal for me was that Dr. Richard O'Brien, the chief of neurology at the Johns Hopkins Bayview Medical Center, gave me generous start-up funds to allow my lab to begin investigating IBM. With formation of a brand-new clinic building at Hopkins Bayview and the warm and intercollegial personality of the Hopkins Bayview Neurology Group led by Dr. Rich O'Brien and Dr. Rafael Llinas, I was sold.

Over the last ten years, my clinical practice has focused on IBM, and I estimate that I have seen about 200 patients with this disease. I was the site principal investigator in the Novartis-sponsored Bimagrumab trial in IBM, and we are now gearing up to start the Arimoclomlol trial. At this point, most of what our clinic has been doing in IBM over the last 10 years is collecting data on patients to better understand the cause of the disease. Our center has enrolled more than 300 IBM patients in a longitudinal database. Each patient has donated blood, DNA, and, in many cases, muscle tissue to our studies. With the advent of high-throughput sequencing technologies and precision medicine initiatives, we are just now on the cusp of really being able to benefit from this wealth of clinical and biological data. We are poised to understand what causes IBM and to finally develop real disease-modifying therapies.

Jim McTevia's story is unique, as is each individual IBM patient's story. Jim is fortunate at this point to be relatively mildly affected, and we do not yet understand why there is such variability in the age of onset and the rate of progression of disease. In writing this afterword, I hope to put Jim's experiences in context with, as best I can, what I have seen as the range of patient experiences over a decade caring for IBM patients. As a disclaimer, I must mention that the majority of patients I continue to see in my clinic are ambulatory, and it's likely that my perspective is skewed by not seeing enough patients who are wheel-chair bound with severe IBM. I believe the reason for this is twofold: the longest I have followed a patient is 10 years; and, once patients lose their ability to walk, the hassle of coming to Baltimore may outweigh the perceived benefits. I'd like to think that our interventions are allowing patients to remain able to walk longer and improve their quality of life, though this would be a claim lacking rigorous scientific evidence. At this point, the best we can do for patient limb weakness is to help them manage their disease with exercise, orthotics, assistive devices, and therapy.

Until we have better scientific evidence for effective treatments in IBM, my general advice is to remain physically active and exercise as much as is safe and feasible. There is excellent scientific evidence that exercise is beneficial with aging in general, including reducing cardiovascular risk and dementia, and as has been the case for Jim, we do see that many IBM patients show at least short-term improvements in muscle function with a regular exercise program. I have learned from my patients how much some of them have benefited from non-weight-bearing resistance exercises such as water aerobics. A stationary bike is likely an excellent way to exercise the leg muscles, and putty or other finger-strengthening exercises are great for maintaining finger flexion strength and flexibility.

Like Jim, many of my IBM patients have found an unconventional therapy that they are convinced has improved their muscle strength or function. As stated in the book, I believe that for untreatable diseases like IBM and ALS, it is very reasonable for patients to try affordable but safe therapies that could potentially provide benefit, even if it is a psychological one. The placebo effect is a well-described and effective therapy; what does it matter if acupuncture, massage, electrical stimulation, vitamins, or herbal remedies are having their beneficial effects on the muscles or on the mind. We know little about what causes IBM and even less about how to treat it, so I am generally supportive of patients trying unproven therapies, though there is a limit.

In the absence of an "evidence-based" approach, patients must rely on their own values and expectations, as well as the advice of their physicians and caretakers. Patients must also be skeptical, though, of questionable alternative therapies such as stem cell injections, chelation therapy, and ketamine infusions. In my opinion, even if cost is not a factor, the risk of these interventions outweighs the potential for a treatment effect. There are good resources available on the Internet to help patients evaluate alternative therapies.

The Myositis Association (myositis.org) has an excellent website and annual conference for patients where they can meet with other patients and myositis specialists to discuss ways of managing their disease. Other good sources of information are cureibm.org (a website maintained by Kevin Dooley, M.D., an ophthalmologist and IBM patient) and the Muscular Dystrophy Association (MDA). There is a website called ALSUntangled.com in which specialists have rigorously investigated alternative therapies tried in ALS and other neuromuscular diseases and discuss potential risks and benefits in an objective and peer-reviewed fashion. I strongly advise caution when getting advice from social media platforms.

I'm often asked about human growth hormone and anabolic steroids. The anabolic steroid oxandrolone has shown a possible benefit in a small clinical trial in IBM, though there are many side effects. The class of muscle building drugs called myostatin inhibitors holds promise for increasing muscle bulk in patients with muscle weakness or atrophy from any cause.

While the Novartis Bimagrumab clinical trial has been reported to be a negative study, there is evidence of an increase in muscle bulk in IBM patients, and Novartis and other companies are developing this class of medications for other indications. Hopefully these drugs will be further tested in IBM, and if approved, there may be a role for them in the management of IBM. In contrast, the over-the-counter supplements currently on the market that are sold as "natural" myostatin inhibitors almost certainly are not biologically active, as the peptide inhibitors would be inactivated in the stomach. Unless supplements become better regulated, I recommend patients be very cautious when taking them.

Likely the best way to test an unproven therapy is in a placebo-controlled, double-blinded clinical trial. Unfortunately, there are not enough of these due to the expense and lack of good drug targets in IBM, but I would strongly encourage all eligible patients to enroll if they can. This is the only way, as a medical community, we can truly learn which therapies are best for IBM patients. I understand Jim's reluctance to take medications given his bad reaction to methotrexate. While toxic side effects of immunosuppressive therapies are rare, the evidence to recommend them in most IBM patients is lacking. For steroids, though, there is good data that long-term treatment with steroids does more harm than good, even though it can improve some symptoms. I'm commonly asked about whether patients can or should take statins. The current evidence suggests that they are safe in IBM, and given the overwhelming evidence for reduction of mortality caused by heart attack or stroke, one must weight any potential side effect against known benefits.

Other than keeping physically active and enrolling in clinical trials, what can individual IBM patients and their loved ones do to accelerate the pace of drug development for IBM? For one thing, the amount of National Institutes of Health (NIH) funding for IBM research per affected patient falls orders of magnitude lower than that for related diseases. In 2013, according to the NIH RePORTER Database, about $8 was spent per IBM patient compared with some $1,838 per patient with Duchenne Muscular Dystrophy, $1,625 per patient with ALS, and $97 per patient with Alzheimer's disease. The relative underfunding of Alzheimer's disease has since been recognized and rectified, but other less common age-related diseases remain woefully underfunded. Thus, patients and their loved ones can work with foundations like the Myositis Association to help increase awareness of this disease and petition federal agencies and private foundations for increased funding for IBM research.

Given the lack of consensus regarding its underlying cause, much more basic research needs to be done to truly understand the etiology of IBM. This should include improving animal models and developing biomarkers. Meanwhile, it is certainly worthwhile to consider clinical trials of drugs in development for related diseases such as Arimoclomol starting this year. I am optimistic that technological advances in biomedical research over the last decade will translate into meaningful treatments for patients in the decade to come.

T.L.

September 2018

ACKNOWLEDGMENTS

⋘⋙

For helping me bring my story to life in these pages, I am grateful to:

My friend Mark Walker, who said I should;

My editor Tom Ferguson and my publisher Bill Haney, who said I could;

My loving family, who knew I would;

And my readers, in the hope they will realize that life is eventually difficult for everyone in one way or another. May they face their adversities one day at a time.

Jim McTevia
Sea Colony
Jupiter, Florida